GOD'S FAITHFULNESS:
A Journey in
TRUSTING
THE LITTLE GIRL FROM THE LOGGING CAMP

Bob McCauley

WESTBOW
PRESS®
A DIVISION OF THOMAS NELSON
& ZONDERVAN

Copyright © 2016 Bob McCauley.

All rights reserved. No part of this book may be used or reproduced by any means, graphic, electronic, or mechanical, including photocopying, recording, taping or by any information storage retrieval system without the written permission of the author except in the case of brief quotations embodied in critical articles and reviews.

This book is a work of non-fiction. Unless otherwise noted, the author and the publisher make no explicit guarantees as to the accuracy of the information contained in this book and in some cases, names of people and places have been altered to protect their privacy.

Scripture taken from the Holy Bible, NEW INTERNATIONAL VERSION®. Copyright © 1973, 1978, 1984 by Biblica, Inc. All rights reserved worldwide. Used by permission. NEW INTERNATIONAL VERSION® and NIV® are registered trademarks of Biblica, Inc. Use of either trademark for the offering of goods or services requires the prior written consent of Biblica US, Inc.

Scripture taken from the King James Version of the Bible.

WestBow Press books may be ordered through booksellers or by contacting:

WestBow Press
A Division of Thomas Nelson & Zondervan
1663 Liberty Drive
Bloomington, IN 47403
www.westbowpress.com
1 (866) 928-1240

Because of the dynamic nature of the Internet, any web addresses or links contained in this book may have changed since publication and may no longer be valid. The views expressed in this work are solely those of the author and do not necessarily reflect the views of the publisher, and the publisher hereby disclaims any responsibility for them.

Any people depicted in stock imagery provided by Thinkstock are models, and such images are being used for illustrative purposes only. Certain stock imagery © Thinkstock.

ISBN: 978-1-5127-2722-7 (sc)
ISBN: 978-1-5127-2723-4 (hc)
ISBN: 978-1-5127-2721-0 (e)

Library of Congress Control Number: 2016900764

Print information available on the last page.

WestBow Press rev. date: 01/20/2016

CONTENTS

Author's Preface vii

Chapter 1. Nailed to the Wall 1
Chapter 2. Logging Camp Life 10
Chapter 3. The Near Drownings 19
Chapter 4. The Wordless Book 28
Chapter 5. To Prairie High School 34
Chapter 6. First Woman to Drive Rogers Pass 39
Chapter 7. Her Father Murdered 42
Chapter 8. Tragedy and God's Blessing 54
Chapter 9. The Proposal 64
Chapter 10. A New Beginning 73
Chapter 11. A New House 78
Chapter 12. Their Daughter's Accident 83
Chapter 13. Aid to Christians in Moscow 89
Chapter 14. Off to Russia 109
Chapter 15. Invited to The Kremlin 113
Chapter 16. Olga's Conversion 118
Chapter 17. The First Public Baptism 123
Chapter 18. Esther's Video Shown on TV 126
Chapter 19. The First Seminary in Moscow 129
Chapter 20. The Roadblock 133
Chapter 21. Off to India 143
Chapter 22. President of Rescue Mission Board 148
Chapter 23. The Last Shipment & Then to The Middle East ... 151
Chapter 24. The Little Russian Girl with Cancer 155

Chapter 25. Ministry to Street Children Begins 161
Chapter 26. Ministering in The Sewer 165
Chapter 27. A Center for Project Hope 171
Chapter 28. "Make it Russian, Make it Russian" 185
Chapter 29. Esther's Wisdom and Bravery 189

AUTHOR'S PREFACE

After the death of my first wife, my children and I went through a time of extreme grief. During this time one of my sons said to me, "Mom was a good person and a missionary so why did God let her die?" He was asking the same question that I was and I did not have a good answer for him. I could clearly remember how my wife and I left good jobs and our beautiful home on a large farm in Indiana and went to Africa as missionaries. I was a senior engineer for a large company and my wife was a teacher. We both felt God was calling us to Africa and we went there in obedience to His call upon our lives. I became a missionary jungle pilot and my wife taught in our mission school. During those years God used both of us to win many people to Jesus Christ. After we were there for five years my wife started to have physical problems and later passed away after we returned to America.

My grief was almost unbearable. Before this I thought I understood those who were going through grief, but I realized I did not. My grief was much worse than I thought it could be. Then, to make matters worse, some of my friends said, "You must have had hidden sin in your life and that is why she died." Others said such things as, "You did not have enough faith or she would have been healed." All of these comments just added to my grief and finally I came to the conclusion that I had to get away from some of my friends who had this type of belief. I purposely did this and spent many weeks in God's Word and prayer seeking the answers to my questions. God was faithful, as He always is, and gave me a deep understanding of how His people can be in His perfect will and still experience tragic events and grief in their lives.

Shortly after my first wife passed away, one of my non-Christian friends said to me, "We are all watching you and now we will see what you are really like." My friends knew I was a Christian and going through grief and some of them were watching to see how I would react. My reaction would reveal to them who I really was and what my faith meant to me. I realized that some of them had talked about this between themselves and were wondering if I would remain a Christian or give up on my faith and return to the life I lived before I accepted Christ as my Savior. As I thought about this I came to the conclusion that there is truth in what he said. It is simply this: we don't know our true character until we are faced with adversity.

In nearly every Christian's life, there are times of grief and suffering of some kind. These difficult times can come upon a Christian through no fault of theirs. When suffering and hardships come, many see no possibility of things improving and see no way God will ever use them in His service again. Also it is very common to question why it is happening to them or to someone they love or know.

God's Faithfulness: A Journey in Trusting is a true story about a woman who was very dedicated to serving the Lord in missions and still went through a very tragic time in her life. This took her out of serving the Lord as a missionary to being nearly penniless with two children to raise. She also felt there was no way she could get out of her situation and work in missions again. Her story stands as an example of God's faithfulness to His people through all of their sufferings. It also shows how God can take two people who have had tragedy in their lives and bring them together through a very unusual romance and use them in His service.

I call this woman, "The little girl from the logging camp." Here is her story.

Chapter 1
NAILED TO THE WALL

Little Esther was a very small eight-year-old child who lived deep in the forest of British Columbia in Western Canada. She was about six inches shorter than most eight-year-olds and very thin. Even though she was a pretty girl, her face had a weathered look from being outside in many cold and windy days. Her dark brown hair had never been cut, so it was down to her shoulders and was usually windblown.

Esther's father, Fred Harasim, was well educated and had worked as a mathematics teacher at one time. When Esther was just a child, her father and mother, Jenny, moved from Alberta to the northern forest of British Columbia and built a logging camp and a sawmill in a very remote area. The camp was located beside a beautiful lake that was surrounded with tall pine, fir and spruce trees. It took about two hours, on a rough mountain road, to get to the nearest town. At the time of this venture, Esther's two brothers were six-year-old Ernie and four-year-old Elmer.

Esther's first language was Ukrainian and she also spoke some Russian. When she first went to school, the teacher told her to go home and learn English before she came back to the first grade. Her family had come to western Canada from the Ukraine and homesteaded in a predominately Ukrainian area in northern Alberta. Neither Esther nor her family knew it at the time but God would greatly use her first language in His service later in her life.

Esther's family lived in the logging camp, along with about fifteen lumberjacks who worked for Fred. For several years, Jenny cooked three large meals every day for the lumberjacks. Their meals included trout from the lake, moose, elk, deer, and sometimes bear. A few of the lumberjacks were married and had their wives and children living with them in very small cabins in the camp. The rest of them lived in a common bunkhouse.

All of the lumberjacks loved Esther, even though they knew she was mischievous at times. She always showed them the highest respect and had a gleam of excitement in her brown eyes, as she talked to them about the things in her forest. She was like their little adopted bush girl who knew the forest better than most of them, even though they worked in it. The men could not help but notice that Esther had understanding and maturity beyond her age.

The outside and inside of the cabins, bunkhouses, and cookhouse were covered with scrap boards that were unfit to sell. The inside of the walls were filled with sawdust for insulation. The cabins usually had only one or two windows, and the glass came from junk cars or trucks. They would frame around a windshield, rear glass, or door glass to make the window. Of course, it would not open.

Usually the cook stove was used to heat the cabins although some had small wood-burning stoves for additional heat. They burned scrap lumber and also used sawdust for their fuel. Even though they had the wood burning stoves, the cabins got very cold during the winter nights, and the water buckets were covered with ice in the morning. Jenny and Fred always got up before the children to prepare a nice hot fire in the wood-burning stove, so it would be warm when the children got up. Then they would break the ice in the water bucket so they could use the water for breakfast. The cabins were built on skids, so they could pull them with bulldozers through the forest if the logging camp relocated. Nothing inside or outside of the buildings was painted, so the general appearance of the camp was not one of beauty, but it was home for little Esther.

For the first year after Esther's parents started the logging camp, Esther, her brother Ernie, and three other children from the logging camp had to walk three miles through the forest to their one-room log schoolhouse. Esther was the oldest of the group, so she felt it was her responsibility to keep her group safe as they made the walk to and from school. Occasionally, they would see wild animals in the forest, and this was always a concern for Esther and her little group. Esther's father had given her specific guidelines for safety as they made the walk. He told her not to worry about the many bears in the forest during the winter because they would be hibernating. He said that the deer were not dangerous, but she had to be very careful of being attacked by a moose.

Fred was concerned for the children because one of his employees had been attacked by a moose. The man was driving a truck loaded with lumber to the train station when he stopped to check his load. He got out of his truck and walked around it to make sure the straps that held the lumber in place were all tight. Suddenly, he heard a noise and quickly turned around, just in time to see a very large bull moose charging at him. He did not even have time to open the door of his truck, but had to jump on top of the truck's hood and climb to the top of the lumber to keep the moose from ramming him with his antlers. The road he was on was in a very remote area, and he had to stay there for a long time until another truck came by and scared the moose away.

Esther's father said they were the most dangerous animals in the forest because they were very aggressive and, many times, would attack and trample a person if they became upset. As a result of her father's warning, little Esther was always on the lookout for a moose as they walked to school in the winter and also for bears in the early fall and spring. She had a special ability to spot a wild animal before it saw her group. When they saw a dangerous animal, they would usually hide behind some trees and wait for the animal to leave the area before they continued on their walk.

During the winter, the ground was covered with at least a foot of snow which made the walk even harder. There was, however, a beauty about the snow-covered forest that Esther loved. Each limb of the evergreen trees was covered with a thick layer of snow, and the bright, green pine needles seemed to almost glow through the white snow on each branch. With the pure white and the bright green throughout the forest, it looked like a beautiful painting that only God could make.

There was also the beauty of the lakes that looked like perfectly level, pure white, open spaces in the forest. At times the children would see a moose near the edge of a frozen lake eating his winter food of twigs from the willow, birch, and poplar shrubs around him. Esther loved the beauty of the northern forest in the winter, even though it could also be very cold.

Sometimes it would be minus forty degrees when the children walked to school so they were all very cold. When they came inside, they would instantly feel the warmth of the homemade heating stove. It was a fifty-five gallon metal barrel lying on its side on a metal stand with a stove pipe coming out of one end and going upward through the roof. At the other end was a metal door for loading logs into the stove. At the top was a flat metal plate welded to the barrel. It was for cooking soup and making hot drinks for the children.

Not only did the children feel the warmth from the stove as they entered the building, but they could also smell the hot cocoa their teacher made for them each morning to help warm them up after their long walk. The children gladly took the cup of tasty cocoa the teacher offered them. Esther loved her school and especially her teacher, who cared deeply for every child. The teacher, a single woman, lived in a very small three-room house next to the school, so she was there early every morning to prepare the hot cocoa and get things ready for the school day.

A teenage boy chopped the wood and kindling for the stove in the schoolhouse. He came by horse early every morning to start the fire in the heating stove, so it would be warm for the children when they arrived. He was also the janitor, so he cleaned the schoolhouse and the outhouse. It was customary for each child to bring cans or packages of soup at the beginning of the week, so the teacher could heat them for their lunches throughout the week. There was a mountain stream about two hundred feet behind the school. Each day one of the children went to the stream and brought back a bucketful of water. The bucket was placed on a small table, along with a dipper for all the children to use when they wanted a drink.

Esther's father knew the three-mile walk in the winter was very difficult for the children, so he decided to do something about it. He bought a horse and had an enclosed sleigh built for them to use when they went to school. The sleigh had a small wood-burning stove in it to keep the children warm, and each child had a blanket to cover up with. However, this did not work well because the horse could not pull the sleigh up the steep hills. He kept slipping and nearly falling so much that the children had to push the sleigh up the hills. In the end, it was much easier for them to make the walk themselves, so they stopped using the horse and sleigh.

When Esther was nine years old, her father built a one-room schoolhouse with a two-room living area in the back for a teacher. He built it about a quarter of a mile away from the camp so there would be less noise from the sawmill. The school board hired a teacher, and the children no longer had to walk three miles to school.

Esther had very few toys or dolls to play with, so the forest and the logging camp she lived in were her play ground. Since the temperature went down to minus forty degrees in the winter, Esther and her friends played outside for long hours when it was zero degrees Fahrenheit because that was not too cold for them. Fred used to give the children the old inner tubes from tires, and they used those as toboggans. He also had some of the men clear a spot on the lake, so the children could skate. Esther spent many hours playing hockey and learning to figure skate.

Even though little Esther was very mature for her age, she occasionally had a mischievous streak. She heard from some of the children in the logging camp that each evening the lumberjacks told very wild stories to each other and that some of their language was quite bad. Esther thought about this for a few days and decided she would like to hear what they talked about in the evenings. Nearly every evening, Esther and her brothers played outside with the other children. Their parents did not worry about them getting into trouble, so they did not keep a close watch on where they were playing. Esther decided to take advantage of this, and one evening she slipped into the bunkhouse and hid under a bed before the lumberjacks came in from their evening meal. From her hiding place, she could listen to them talking.

Soon, the lumberjacks returned to their bunkhouse, and they had hardly started to talk when one of them sat down on the bed that little Esther was under. The middle of the bed sank down from his weight, and the bedsprings hit Esther's back very hard. She let out a yell, and the lumberjacks were shocked to see the little stow-away hiding under the bed. They quickly pulled her out, and without even asking her a question, decided to teach her a lesson.

One of them lifted her up by the back of her brand new winter coat and held her about four feet high against the inside bunkhouse wall. Another took a hammer and a large nail and drove it through the back of her coat into the wooden wall. Then they left little, nosy Esther hanging on the nail. Probably they would have taken her down after a few minutes, but they did not have to. Esther started to kick and try to pull herself off of the nail so much that her coat tore, and she fell to the floor after about thirty seconds.

Then she ran out the door and back to the little two-room cabin where her family lived. She did not say a word to her mother about what had just happened, but within minutes, her mother saw the large tear in her brand new coat and asked about it. Esther knew she had done something very wrong, and her mother would be very angry with her when she found out. With tears in her eyes and her heart breaking, Esther confessed to her mother what she had done and what the men did after they discovered her in their bunkhouse under the bed.

Her mother did not blame the lumberjacks at all, but put the full blame on Esther. She knew Esther loved her new coat very much and was very proud to wear it, but she decided to teach her a lesson and made her wear it until it no longer fit; however, she did mend the tear. It was the only coat Esther had, and it would be at least two years before she outgrew it. That was to be her punishment, and Esther learned a very valuable lesson. She learned that many times in life people have to live with the results of the wrong things they have done. She was reminded of this each time she put on the coat. It was a lesson that stayed with her the rest of her life.

Even as the little girl from the logging camp was learning the long-term results of sneaking into the lumberjacks' cabin, she still had a little streak of mischief in her heart. She did not blame the lumberjacks for what they did to her, but she did want to get even with them. Her motive for wanting to get even was not anger. She loved them too much for that. It was like a game to Esther, and the lumberjacks had one up on her. Now she had to get one on them. Of course, she told all of the other children about getting nailed to the wall, and that she wanted to get even with the lumberjacks. Every one of them agreed with her, and they wanted to help.

After thinking about it for few days, Esther's little gang came up with a plan. They would smoke the lumberjacks out of their bunkhouse. They just had to work out the details of how to do it. Esther knew they had a fire going in their heating stove every day, so if they could stop the smoke from coming out of the chimney, the whole bunkhouse would quickly fill with smoke. Since the fire was burning all day, they would have to wait to stop the smoke from coming out of the chimney until all of the men had returned to the bunkhouse after their supper. They could do this. Little Esther was excited about their plan and was confident it would work well.

After dark the next evening, Esther and her gang carried a long ladder to the bunkhouse while the men were eating in the lumberjacks' cookhouse. They placed the ladder up against the end of the bunkhouse where the chimney was and waited for the men to return to the bunkhouse. After all of the men were back, one of the bigger boys very quietly climbed the ladder, placed a short board over the chimney, and quickly climbed back down.

The chimney was on the opposite end of the bunkhouse from the door, so Esther's gang ran to the other end and up to the door. The door had a homemade inside latch and two bent nails on the outside to hold it closed. They turned the two bent nails over the edge of the door and locked it from the outside. Then they ran and hid behind some bushes. From their location, they could easily hear the men inside and watch when they tried to run out.

Surprisingly enough, the plan worked perfectly! They started giggling and laughing as quietly as they could as they watched. Soon they heard the men start to yell, using some rather graphic language, stating that the room was filling with smoke. By this time, the children were laughing so hard they could hardly hold back the noise. They were proud of themselves for their success. Then they heard the lumberjacks pushing and ramming against the door in an effort to open it.

The two bent nails were holding the door closed longer than they expected. The little villains were very excited as they watched the door being rammed out a little but not opening. By this time, the villains were laughing so hard that they did not even try to hold it back to stop anyone from hearing. In about two minutes, the bent nails came out. The door swung open, and out ran the coughing and confused lumberjacks.

Their confusion over what happened to cause the smoke to fill the room soon turned into laughter as they looked up at the board covering their chimney. They all knew immediately that Esther had pulled a fast one on them to get even for nailing her to the wall. Quickly, they climbed the ladder that Esther and her gang used and removed the board. Within fifteen minutes the smoke was out of the bunkhouse and the lumberjacks went back inside. They were a good bunch of guys who took the whole thing as a joke on them. They even admired the ingenuity and ability it took for Esther to pull it off. It was fun for Esther and her gang, and in the end, it was even fun for the men who experienced the smoke filled room!

Chapter 2
LOGGING CAMP LIFE

Even though the logging camp was in the forest, it was not a quiet place. During the day there was the constant sound of the large diesel engines that drove the sawmill equipment, bulldozers, trucks and other logging equipment. During the very cold winter nights they did not shut off the diesel engines because it was very difficult to start them in the minus forty-degree weather. As a result, there was a continuous sound of motors running day and night in the winter.

There were other sounds during the night that little Esther heard. There was the sound of the coyotes and wolves howling throughout the night. She could hear them above the sound of the engines running. At times it sounded like they were howling right outside the camp. Then again, it sounded like a pack howling miles away. Their howl echoed throughout the forest, and it was a very eerie sound. Sometimes it sounded like they were sad and wanting help. At other times, it sounded like they were talking to other packs that were far away. There had to be hundreds out there.

Although Esther heard so many of them, she hardly ever saw one when she was walking to school. After hearing their howls all night, she knew they were there during the day and probably watching her and the other children as they walked to and from school. She knew that she had to be very careful.

The lumberjacks' work was hard and very dangerous. As much as they tried to stop accidents, there were still times when someone got badly hurt. One time a man's legs were cut off, and another time a man was killed when a log rolled down a hill and over him. Esther's father had first aid supplies in the camp that they used successfully for most of the injuries. However, if someone was hurt bad enough to need a doctor or needed to go to the hospital, he would call out on his two way radio and ask for a doctor to fly in. In the winter the doctor flew in and landed on the frozen lake with a ski plane. In the summer he came in on a plane with floats and landed on the water. For all other ailments, such as colds, mumps, etc., they just took care of it themselves.

Esther's father was an extremely busy man, managing the lumberjacks, running the equipment and trucks when needed, traveling to find sales for his lumber, purchasing supplies for the camp, as well as being a father and husband. It was a constant effort to run the camp efficiently enough to make a profit on the lumber. The payroll for the lumberjacks was very high. At times, Fred hardly had enough money to pay them, so his own family had to go without many of the things they needed.

To make the business profitable, the whole family worked hard. Esther's brothers Ernie and Elmer stacked lumber so it could dry. They also chopped and carried wood to the house for the cooking stove, as well as for heat. All three children took turns carrying water to the house from the lake. Esther helped her mother cook for the lumberjacks. It was a big job, and she learned to work hard, even as a small girl.

From about the first of October until Easter there was too much snow on the roads for small trucks and cars to get to town. Only the big logging trucks could get out. As a result, everyone in the logging camp, except the truck drivers, had to remain there through the winter months. The truck drivers picked up the mail and brought back food and other supplies when they took lumber into town. There were no telephones, TVs or newspapers in the camp and radio reception was nearly impossible. Consequently, contact with the outside world was very limited. When Esther's father went to town with one of the logging trucks, he always brought back news of what was happening in the world.

Fred also had a secret job that few knew about. He was a secret agent for the Canadian Government and was helping them investigate the Communist Party, which was developing in Canada at that time. Fred attended most of their meetings pretending to be one of them; then he gave the details of their plans to the Canadian Government. It was a very dangerous job because he or his family could have suffered serious retaliations against them if the Communist Party found out about it.

Even though Fred tried to keep it a secret, Jenny found out what he was doing and did not like it one bit. She was very fearful for his life as well as for her family and did not want him to continue doing it. Fred did not like what the Communists were trying to do in his country and felt what he was doing was very vital in stopping it. As a result, he refused to stop. This caused some very tense arguments between Fred and Jenny.

One time they were arguing about this and didn't realize little seven-year-old Esther was listening to every word. She did not know anything about the Communist Party, but after hearing her father describe the importance of what he was doing, she believed he was helping Canada, and she would keep his secret. One evening Fred went to one of the meetings and took Esther with him. When they walked into the meeting room, some of the people seemed surprised that he brought his little daughter. Then Fred introduced her to all of them and they appeared to be happy that he felt free to bring her.

After the introduction, Fred had Esther sit in a chair in a room next to where they were meeting. Even though she was sitting outside of the meeting room, she could hear every word, but she could not understand what they were talking about. It was just too complicated for her. As little Esther sat there, she thought again about what her father was doing and knew it was very important. Yes, she would keep his secret and not tell any of her friends or anyone else about it

During this time in her life, Esther's father taught her to shoot his 30.06-hunting rifle. He was a very good shot and it was a valuable skill in getting meat for his family and the lumberjacks. They had little access to beef or pork, so they had to live on meat they could get from the forest, such as moose, elk, deer and bear. Esther's father felt that being able to shoot a rifle well was not just a skill for boys and men, but it was important for girls and women also. He taught Esther's mother how to shoot his rifle and she could shoot quite well.

Fred knew his little Esther was not strong enough to hold the barrel up to shoot his rifle, so he taught her how to lay the barrel on some kind of support, such as a post or a tree limb, and then aim and shoot. Fred also taught Esther how to make adjustments for wind and elevation and also how to slowly pull the trigger so that her aim stayed exactly where she wanted it when the gun fired.

It did not take long for Esther to become very good at shooting. She was so small that the kick of the 30.06 really jolted her in the beginning. Her shoulder even hurt some from the kick, but soon she got used to it and in time she hardly noticed it. She became so good at shooting that her father encouraged her to enter a shooting contest that was being held nearby. After a little coaxing from her father, she entered the contest and did very well. She won first prize!

Bears were often a problem in the forest. People who lived there knew that a 400- pound bear could run over thirty miles an hour. A man could not outrun them and very few animals could. Sometimes one would become very aggressive and start killing the rancher's cows. Sometimes they even killed grown men. Once, a bear killed a man in the forest. Then one of his friends went out by himself with a high-powered rifle in an attempt to find and kill the bear. The bear attacked the man and killed him even though he had the rifle. After the second man was killed, two more men went out with rifles to find the bear and kill it. They looked for a long time and could not find him, so they split up in an attempt to cover more ground to find the bear.

One of the men suddenly heard a shot and ran in the direction of the noise thinking his friend had killed the bear. Suddenly he saw the bear standing over his friend. The man took good aim and shot the bear. Then he ran to where the bear was and saw that his friend was dead. Bears are very clever animals, and sometimes if a person is following them, they will circle around and come up behind the person and kill them. The man who finally killed the bear saw that this was what happened to his friend.

One day, some of the men saw evidence that a bear was coming into the camp during the night. Fred and the lumberjacks knew this was very dangerous, especially when there were children in the camp. Every evening the children played outside after it was dark. The possibility of a bear attacking one of them was a concern to Fred and everyone in the camp. Fred and his men knew they had to do something about it. Esther's Uncle Billy and Uncle Peter worked for Fred, and they agreed to stay up all night and watch for the bear. They decided to sit in a truck through the nights and wait for it to show up.

One of them stayed awake all night and watched, and the next night the other stayed awake. On the third night Esther's Uncle Billy was watching from the truck. Then he saw it! A very large black bear was walking through the camp. Billy had his high-powered rifle ready. He slowly took aim in the dark and pulled the trigger. The 30.06 made a very loud noise as it fired, and the bear dropped dead instantly. The gunshot woke everyone in the camp, and they ran out to see the big black bear lying dead near the center of the camp. Everyone was happy, especially Fred! They had removed a dangerous animal from the camp. The next morning some of the lumberjacks skinned the bear and cut it up for eating. They put the meat in the icehouse, and every few days Jenny would serve some of it to them for their meals.

Esther's family really enjoyed having a good beef roast. One day Jenny cooked a large one for their dinner and put it out to cool on a tall bench on the back porch while she prepared the rest of the meal. After a while she went to get the roast thinking it probably had cooled enough to serve. She could hardly believe her eyes. The roast was gone! She looked around wondering where it was and then she saw it. A black bear was holding it between his paws devouring it. Jenny was not happy with that bear at all.

Jenny had prepared that roast for her family's dinner, and here the bear had quietly come up to her porch and took it off of the plate without her hearing anything at all. Besides being upset that her roast was gone, Jenny did not like it that a bear had become a visitor at her house. She knew this was a dangerous situation, so she decided to shoot the bear. She knew how to shoot Fred's 30.06 rifle, but Esther's younger brother Elmer also knew how to shoot the rifle. He wanted to be the one to do it so he went outside with his father's rifle, took aim and shot the bear. They skinned the bear and had roast bear a few days later.

Esther's long walk to school put her in the area of dangerous animals such as bears, mountain lions, wild cats, wolves and moose. She constantly knew if she was not very careful these animals could easily kill her. She had heard many stories of grown men being killed by them. Then on top of that, she knew that every time she went into the forest, she was in their territory. Little Esther could have reacted to this danger with extreme fear, but she refused to do that.

She knew the area was also her territory. She lived there and she was not going to live in fear. Esther would respect and understand the animals and do all she could do to protect her friends, brothers and herself. This attitude was developed so early in little Esther that by the time she was nine years old, it was a deep part of her character.

By this time in life, Esther had learned to make decisions based on logic rather than emotions. For example, what would she do if she saw a bear before it saw her? If her emotions took over she might scream, which would alert the bear to where she was, and this could cost her life. One day she did come upon a bear about fifty feet in front of her. The bear was eating something and did not see Esther. She did not scream, but quickly hid herself the best she could and decided how to get out of this dangerous situation.

She knew if the bear walked in her direction he would see her, and the results could be tragic. She also knew that bears cannot see very far, but they can hear very well. Using this knowledge, she slowly bent over, picked up a rock, and threw it as far as she could in a direction away from her. The bear heard the rock hit the ground and took off after it, giving her time to get away. Esther's logic told her that the bear would go in the direction of the sound of the rock hitting the ground and gladly it did!

Esther, her brothers and the other camp kids also chose something for entertainment that was very dangerous. Their parents would have stopped it immediately if they had known what the children were doing. There was a very large pile of sawdust in the camp that was at least as big as a two-story house. The children started digging long tunnels back into the pile of sawdust. When they dug a tunnel about five or six feet long, they would use scraps of lumber from the sawmill for braces so the sawdust would not cave in. Then they would dig deeper until they finally had many tunnels and even small rooms in the sawdust pile. When their parents found out about it, they were very upset. They knew the tunnels could have caved in, and the children would have suffocated before anyone could find them.

Esther's mother and father and the three children slept in a very small bedroom in their two-room cabin. The three children all slept in one double bed and their parents in another. The beds were each against an outside wall with about six or seven feet between them. Between the beds and against an outside wall, was a dresser. At the end of each bed there was a makeshift closet and some shelves covered by curtains. The room was very crowded, yet they lived like that for several years. When Esther was about eleven years old, her mother decided it was time she had her own room, so she made one for her.

Jenny used 2x4 inch studs making a six by six foot room in the corner of the kitchen and living room. Then she nailed pieces of cardboard on the studs to finish the walls. Of course there were no windows, but the walls were only six feet high, so light and air could come from the top. A curtain covered the doorway for privacy. Jenny then took some old orange crate boxes, covered them with cloth, and made Esther a dresser. The room was very rustic, but it never entered Esther's mind how common and rustic it was. It was her own room, and she was proud of it.

All the drinking water for the entire camp came from the nearby lake. By the middle of October when the lake had frozen over, they had to chop a hole in the ice to dip out their water. As the winter went on, the ice got thicker. By mid-November they had to use a chain saw to cut the hole deeper. By December the temperature usually dropped down to minus forty degrees and the ice was three feet thick. Every day the lumberjacks had the difficult job of cutting out the ice to keep the hole open, so the camp could get their water.

It was difficult to stand next to the open hole, throw a bucket down with a rope tied to it, let it fill with water and lift it out. At times, there were small fish in the bucket of water when they pulled it up. Rather than throwing the water away, they just dipped the fish out and used the water. Nobody ever became ill from drinking the lake water.

The family took a bath once a week in a very small fold up canvas tub. After their weekly baths, they emptied the water, folded the tub and stored it under a bed. It was difficult to heat enough water for a bath, so the children used the same water for their baths. Jenny decided that since Esther was a girl, she should enjoy the privilege of having the first bath (also because she was the cleanest and the water would still be clean for the boys). This caused problems between Esther and her two brothers. Elmer and Ernest did not like this process at all and complained to their mother that it was not fair that Esther always got the first bath. Jenny did not give in an inch and little Esther always had the first bath.

One day, however, Esther disobeyed her mother and Jenny said, "Because you disobeyed, tonight you will have the last bath." Well, that was one of the worst punishments Esther's mother could have given her. By the time she had her bath the water was cold, the bottom of the tub had sand and dirt in it and the water was just plain dirty! Esther felt like she had not even had a bath; she felt just as dirty after her bath as she had before the bath. This lesson should have caused Esther to obey her mother in everything. However, it did not always work that way, especially when it meant she might miss out on fun and an adventure.

Chapter 3
THE NEAR DROWNINGS

Warm summer days in northern British Columbia were very few. Even though little nine-year-old Esther lived right beside the lake, she had only a few days warm enough to go swimming. As a result she did not learn how swim, but loved to play in the water when she could, along with the other children from the logging camp. One summer day Esther's mother and father left the camp to take care of some business. Before they left, Esther's mother gave her strict instructions, "Don't go swimming while we are gone!" Esther clearly heard her mother's instructions, but as the day rolled on, it became warm enough to swim and some of the children were already in the water. Little Esther sat on the bank and watched the children having so much fun. She wished she could play in the water with them.

Finally, after several minutes of watching the children and feeling kind of "left out," she started to reason, "Mom and Dad are gone and they will not know if I go out and play in the water." This reasoning finally won out over the instructions from Esther's mother. She quickly put on her bathing suit and ran into the water as fast as she could. She did not want to miss out on any of the action.

There was an inner tube from a very large piece of logging equipment lying on the bank. Esther grabbed it, pulled it into the water and tried to lie across it and float around splashing the other children. The inside opening was so large that her body could hardly reach across the inside diameter and her arms were not long enough to reach around the tube. She was struggling to hold onto the tube and splash the other children at the same time.

Little Esther was having fun, but was slowly drifting away from the bank. The water gradually got deeper for the first forty feet from the bank, but then it suddenly dropped off into extremely deep water. Esther knew this, but she was having so much fun that she did not notice she was out far enough to be over the edge of the drop off.

It was quitting time in the evening for the lumberjacks and they had shut down the machines and were walking back to their bunkhouse. Three of the men stopped for a few minutes to watch the children swimming and having fun in the water. They saw little Esther splashing water at a boy and he was doing the same to her. However, he was standing in the shallow part of the water and Esther was in her tube over the drop off. Then the men suddenly realized she had disappeared, and the tube was floating by itself! They knew little Esther had fallen off her tube and had not come back up. Immediately they knew they had to save her because she had gone down into the very deep drop off. The men instantly pulled off their logging boots and ran towards the area where they last saw little Esther.

When Esther lost her grip on the inside diameter of the inner tube she tried to grab the outside, but she could not hold on. Almost instantly, she felt herself descending straight down below the water's surface. She was holding her breath with her eyes open as she descended deeper and deeper. She could see the fish swimming around her as she was going down, but she did not know how to make herself go back up. Soon she was in the green weeds and she could see them and the fish very clearly. Her lungs were almost bursting for air and she could not hold on any longer without taking a breath. She knew she was going to drown. Suddenly she felt a strong pull on her hair and then everything went black.

The first man into the water was a nineteen-year-old lumberjack who worked for Fred. He ran as fast as he could towards the drop off and then dove under. He still had on his heavy logging clothes and found it difficult to quickly swim downward because they were catching the water and holding him back. He had his eyes open and found that the water was murky because of the dirt that the children had stirred up when they were playing. As he got deeper, the water cleared up and he could see much better.

He was surprised at how deep the water was at the drop off. He had never swum down that deep before, but he would not give up. His lungs started to feel like they were going to explode from the lack of air, but he kept going. Then, to his surprise, he saw the top of Esther's head and her hair floating above her. He reached out, grabbed her hair, and held on tight, swimming towards the surface as fast as he could.

When he reached the top, he gasped for air and quickly lifted little Esther's head above the water. Immediately, the other lumberjacks' strong hands grabbed and lifted them above the water. After a few heavy breaths, the young man who rescued Esther gained his strength back and was able to swim out. But little Esther was not responding. They quickly carried her to the bank, laid her on her stomach and gave her artificial respiration. Within a few seconds, some water came out of her mouth and she started to cough repeatedly. One of the men ran to the bunkhouse and got a blanket and wrapped it around her.

Esther finally stopped coughing and opened her eyes. When her eyes started to focus, she saw several lumberjacks and children gazing down at her. They all had very serious looks on their faces, but when they saw Esther looking at them, they all started to smile. They realized the seriousness of what had just happened and they were so happy that their little Esther, whom they all loved, was going to be okay. Little Esther was so thankful for what they had done to save her. She was especially thankful to the lumberjack who had rescued her. She knew if he had not put out a very special effort she would have been dead.

Then it hit Esther! She would be in big trouble with her mother. She had disobeyed her by going swimming. Esther could hardly face the thought of her mother finding out what had happened and she started to panic. "Please, please don't tell my mom," she cried. They all honored Esther's request, and the incident was dropped, both by the lumberjacks and the children.

About sixty years later, not long before her mother passed away, Esther told her mother the secret that she had held back from her all of those years. Jenny was surprised but did not get upset and was thankful that her little Esther's life was saved.

There was something about living in a logging camp beside a beautiful lake that made every day like an adventure for little Esther and her brothers. The adventure could range from watching an eagle swoop down and pick up a fish to playing cowboys and Indians in the forest with all sorts of things in between. Every day was like a happening for them and they preferred no other place in the world to live.

The combination of a dangerous place such as a logging camp and children who did not always obey their parents was the perfect breeding ground for serious problems. Disobeying her mother's orders was not uncommon for little Esther and her brothers, especially if obedience meant missing out on some adventure. One day they decided to try out a new adventure and got into trouble for disobeying. This time it was Ernie, Esther's oldest brother, who nearly drowned.

Fred had a lease from the Canadian government for the timber around the lake they lived on. The lease also included a large area along the river that flowed into the lake. The easiest way to get the logs to the logging camp was to float them downstream and across the lake to the sawmill. When they floated the logs to the camp, they connected many of them together into what is called a log boom. To make a log boom, they chained very long logs end for end, and this made a floating fence. They put the shorter logs inside the floating fence and then connected a motor boat to the outer long logs and pulled the large boom of logs to the camp.

When they were floating the logs, there were usually men with long poles standing on the logs in the boom. It was their job to move the logs in certain ways to stop a logjam. This was very dangerous work because the logs could easily roll in the water and a man could fall off. If a man fell between two logs, his weight usually pushed the logs apart just far enough for him to drop into the water between them. The logs would then come back together when the man was under water. Then it was nearly impossible for the man to push the logs apart enough to get his head out of the water and he could drown. If a man did fall in, he needed to have one or two other men who could quickly push the logs apart enough for him to get out. Some of these men became very skilled, and that is how the logrolling contest started.

On a Saturday when the logging operation was shut down for the weekend, Esther, Ernie and Elmer, along with some of the other boys, were playing in the camp when someone suggested they go down to the log boom area. All the children knew it was strictly against Fred's rules for any child to go near the log boom. One of them said that the log boom area was out of sight of the bunkhouse and cabins where all of the adults were, so they would not be caught if they went there. They all agreed and took off running. Soon they arrived on the bank where the log boom was floating in the lake.

Little Esther stopped at the top of the bank, but the boys ran right to the edge of the water. As seven-year-old Ernie stood at the water's edge looking at the floating logs, he thought about the stories he had heard about the expert log rollers who competed in the logrolling contest. He thought for a little bit and said to himself, "I can do that." Then he challenged one of his friends to a contest to see who could roll a log the fastest. The friend agreed and Ernie was the first to run out on the floating logs and try rolling one by running on top of it.

Esther was not close enough to Ernie and his friend to hear their plan. Suddenly she saw Ernie run across the logs. She was shocked and knew it was very dangerous, but it was too late to stop him. She saw him try to roll a log, but almost immediately he slipped and fell between two of them. When he fell, the logs moved apart just enough for his body to slide between them and down into the water. Instantly, the logs came back together with no space at all between them.

Ernie was suddenly in a dire situation that had caused the death of many lumberjacks! He could not surface to breathe, and no matter how hard he tried, he could not push the logs apart. He was holding his breath, but his lungs were crying out for air. He had never held his breath this long, and he could not do it much longer. He knew death was very close, and he was extremely afraid.

The children all saw Ernie go under, and knew he would drown if they did not do something quickly. There was no adult who could get there in time to help. They had to do it! Little Esther was shouting orders to the boys who were closer to Ernie, telling them what to do. Next to where the boys were standing were some poles the lumberjacks used to move the logs in the boom. They were special poles with hooks on them to keep logs from rolling.

Two older boys each grabbed a pole and ran out to the floating logs that were holding Ernie down. They had never done this before and they knew they also could fall between the logs as Ernie had. Undeterred by this thought, they skillfully pried the two logs apart enough that Ernie was able to get his head above the water and get a breath of air.

The boys then kept the logs from rolling as Ernie climbed up out of the water and on top of one of them. Doing all of this would have been a big job for any man, but these two young boys did it. After Ernie got on top of one of the logs, the boys let them come back together. Then they helped Ernie carefully crawl across the logs back to the bank.

All the children knew that Ernie had come close to drowning and they knew it happened because they had disobeyed Fred's orders for them not to go near the log boom. Esther took it the hardest. She knew that as the oldest it was her responsibility to protect her brothers and the other children and she had failed terribly. She should have spoken out and taken a stand that they were not to go against her father's orders. She was heartbroken that she had not.

Esther was so glad that Ernie was alive and that the boys had rescued him from sure death. She loved all those children, especially her brothers, and did not want them to be hurt in any way. As a result, she made a decision that she would do a better job of protecting them in the future. It was a good decision, made with good intent, but as a nine-year-old, she did not always stick to it as she thought she would.

Ernie was all wet when they returned to the cabin. His parents immediately wanted to know why. As much as Ernie and little Esther hated to confess their disobedience, they told their parents the full story. Their mother and father were very upset about them being disobedient, but they were so happy that Ernie was still alive that they did not punish Ernie or Esther. They figured the results of their disobedience were so traumatic that it taught them a lesson they would never forget.

The winters in the northern forest were very long, providing a long time for winter fun. When the children were not working or in school, they spent a lot of time skating and playing hockey on the frozen lake. There was one danger of skating on the lake that many did not realize. A river flowed into the lake on one end and exited on the other end. As a result, the water level was constantly changing both in the summer and winter. It all depended on how much water was flowing into the lake and how much was flowing out.

This constant change in the water level often caused the ice to have what the local people called "air pockets." The ice over an air pocket was much thinner than the ice in other parts of the lake, causing the ice over the air pocket to have a white crusty look that could be distinguished if a person looked closely. They were usually only a few feet in diameter, but dangerous because the ice over them was not strong enough to hold a person.

One day when the ice had frozen enough for skating, Esther and some of the other children decided they wanted to skate all the way around the lake. Esther asked her mother for permission and Jenny said she could go if she skated right next to the bank all the way around. She wanted Esther to skate next to the bank in case the ice broke, and she fell in. The water next to the edge would be very shallow, and she could easily get out. Esther was excited about being allowed to go, so she and a few of the other children quickly left to go skating. It was about three miles around the lake and all the children were staying right next to the bank going as fast as they could.

They should have been pacing themselves to skate the three miles, but they did not think that far ahead. After about one mile, Esther said she was getting tired. Some of the other children also said they were getting tired and after about another mile, all of the children said they were tired. One of the children suggested they cut across the lake towards the camp. It was only about a quarter of a mile that way and they still had at least another mile or maybe more, to get all the way around the edge of the lake. They all agreed to take the shortcut and headed directly across the lake to the camp.

Little Esther was happily anticipating getting back to her camp where she could rest and get warmed up. Then it happened! She skated over an air pocket, the ice broke instantly and she fell through the ice. Almost all of Sharps Lake was very deep, but there was a small area where Esther fell through that was shallow, so her feet hit the bottom before her head went under the ice. This was a blessing of God for Esther because she could have gone on down and drowned. The other skaters immediately stopped and two of the boys took hold of Esther arms and lifted her back on the ice.

They did not even take time to talk, but skated towards the camp as fast as they could. Esther's clothes started to freeze and became stiff as she was skating. She was so cold she could hardly skate but kept going with every ounce of strength she had left. Finally she reached the bank along with the other children. With her skates still on, she ran to her cabin and immediately went in and sat down in front of their heating stove.

Quickly her mother removed all her wet clothes, including her skates, and put a bathrobe around her. She let her sit near the stove to warm up. Jenny ran outside, got a bucket of snow and rubbed Esther's cheeks and feet with the snow to help bring back the circulation. She didn't want Esther to warm up too quickly, as that was not good; it was best to warm up slowly in case of severe frostbite. How thankful they were that she didn't have any lasting effects from the bitter cold that she had endured that day.

Chapter 4
THE WORDLESS BOOK

One day two missionary women from England drove an old Volkswagen van a long way down some very difficult roads to get to the little log school house Esther attended. When they came into the school, they introduced themselves and asked the teacher for permission to talk to the children. The teacher was happy to have them teach for the afternoon as it gave her a little break and gave the children an opportunity to hear someone besides her. The children were excited as well because they seldom had visitors. Nobody had ever come to their school and asked to talk to them before. It also meant that they wouldn't have to do their lessons that afternoon!

The missionaries had a little book called *The Wordless Book*. It had blank pages of several different colors. The children had never seen such a book before and were very interested in hearing about it. The two women told the children that the color of each page had a special meaning that they wanted to talk to them about. The first page was black, representing sin and the women told the children that all had sinned and that God hated sin. Then they quoted two verses in the Bible that really spoke to little Esther.

Romans 3:23 for all have sinned and fall short of the glory of God, (NIV)

Luke 13:3 I tell you, no! But unless you repent, you too will all perish. (NIV)

The next page was red, and the women explained that Jesus died for their sins and paid for them by His blood. The women also quoted two more verses that spoke to little Esther's heart.

John 3:16 For God so loved the world that he gave his one and only Son, that whoever believes in him shall not perish but have eternal life.(NIV)

John 3:3 *Jesus replied, "Very truly I tell you, no one can see the kingdom of God unless they are born again."(NIV)*

The third page, which was white, explained that they could be clean and free from sin if they accepted Jesus as Lord and Savior. The fourth page was green indicating that they should grow in their service to God through Jesus Christ. The gold page represented the beauty and wonderful things in Heaven where people would someday go if they had repented and accepted Jesus as their Savior. When Esther heard this story, she knew she had sinned and was like the black page. She wanted to ask God to forgive her and to accept His Son as the Sacrifice for her sins. The women asked the children to raise their hand if they wanted to accept Jesus, and Esther immediately did.

The children who raised their hands were led in prayer by one of the women. They asked Jesus to come into their hearts and take away their sins. Each child who accepted the Lord also received a copy of the book of John. As soon as Esther prayed, she felt clean inside. She knew God had forgiven her. Something very sacred happened in her. As a little nine-year-old she could not explain it, but she knew it happened. She felt like she had been born again just as the Scripture said a person had to be before they could enter Heaven. Little Esther knew if she died she would go to that beautiful place.

After the lesson and praying with those who accepted Jesus as their Savior, the two women got back in their old van and drove off. Little Esther never saw them again, but what happened that day was a life-changing event for her. After that day, her whole lifestyle changed;

although she still wanted to have fun and adventure, now she wanted to be a witness for Jesus Christ.

That day was the beginning of a series of events in which God would greatly use little Esther as his servant to win hundreds of people to a life changing born again experience through God's Son, Jesus Christ. Esther did not know it at that time, but Satan was going to throw tragic events into her life in an effort to distract or stop her from accomplishing what God had planned for her. Her faith would be greatly tested in the years to come and how she responded would make a great difference to her ministry in the future.

Not long after this, Esther's parents decided to send her to visit her grandparents who lived in Glendon, Alberta. Esther was born in that area and spent the first four years of her life there. Fred and Jenny took Esther to the train station in the very small town of Ashcroft. When the train arrived, they told the conductor where Esther was going and put her in his charge. For the next two and a half days, Esther rode the train through the mountains. When the train arrived in Glendon, the conductor told Esther it was time to get off. When she got off of the train, her grandparents were waiting for her. It was an exciting reunion for Esther, as she had not seen them for a couple of years. She also had aunts, uncles, and cousins who lived in or near Glendon, and she got to see all of them, making her time there very special.

Esther's grandmother took her to a little Ukrainian church on Sunday and she saw something that excited her. It was a box of children's old Sunday school papers and teacher's manuals. Shortly after Esther accepted the Lord Jesus as her Savior, she wanted to tell others about Him. She wanted to have a little Sunday school class in the camp, but she did not have any teaching materials; this box of papers and manuals would be perfect for her to use. She told the teacher what she wanted to do and asked if she could have the papers and books. The Sunday school teacher was happy for Esther to take them.

When it came time for Esther to return to the logging camp, she filled her suitcase with as many books as she could and her grandparents took her to the train. Before she got on, she hugged and kissed them goodbye. She knew it could be a long time before she saw them again. With a few tears in her eyes, she climbed up the two steps into the train car and took her seat in a location where she could see her grandparents. When the train started to roll away, she waved goodbye.

As little Esther was making the two and a half day ride by herself back to Ashcroft, she kept thinking about the missionary women who came to her school. There was something special about them. She could see that the women had a love for others that caused them to come all of the way from England to British Columbia and then make a long hard drive on the rough mountain roads to their schoolhouse to tell the children about Jesus. At the young age of nine, little Esther made a decision that became a goal in her life. It was to become a missionary and go to foreign countries and tell people about Jesus Christ.

Shortly after little Esther got back to the logging camp, with no help from the adults, she started her Sunday school class. Even though she was only nine years old, she became very dedicated to studying the materials and being prepared for each of her classes, which she held in her parents cabin. There were about eight children from the logging camp and they all gladly attended the Sunday school. Even the parents appreciated what she was doing to help their children learn about God and the Bible.

Esther tried to teach her Sunday school class exactly as it was done in her grandparents' church. This included giving her lesson and having communion using water and pieces of bread. Then she had a collection just like the church did. When the children came to Sunday school, they each brought a small amount of money and put it in the collection plate that Esther passed around. Esther was not sure what the money was for, so she gave it to her father and asked him to "find what to do with it."

As time went on, Fred ended up with a few dollars that Esther had given him to hold and he did not know what to do with the money either. Then he remembered a little magazine called *The Prairie Overcomer* that Jenny's Christian aunt sent to them; it was from Prairie Bible Institute and he remembered that it was located about a two hour drive from where he grew up on a farm near Two Hills, Alberta. After thinking about it, he added several dollars and sent the money to them. When the institute received the money, they sent some Christian materials to Fred, which became a blessing to the whole family.

Esther's dedication to God's ministry became an overwhelming part of her character by the time she was ready for high school. Her parents saw that she had a desire for the things of God and even though they weren't living for the Lord themselves, they had a great respect for Christianity. They encouraged Esther to go to Prairie Bible Institute to attend high school. When they first approached the subject with Esther, she felt overwhelmed at the idea. Prairie was several hundred miles away in another province. In some ways she knew she wanted to go, and in other ways, she hated to leave the Caribou, the area where she grew up.

The Caribou had everything she loved so much. The beautiful mountains and lakes, the tall evergreen trees, the streams and rivers winding through the mountains, the wild animals and birds and all the beauty of nature that she had grown to love. But, at the very top of her list would be leaving her mother, father and brothers whom she loved very much. She was only thirteen at the time yet mature enough to know she needed and wanted a good education.

Her commitment to Christ and wanting to be used of God as a missionary was somewhat fulfilled when she became a Sunday school teacher to the children in the logging camp. Now she could no longer do that because her father's contract with the Canadian government for the lumber at Sharps Lake had finished and the lumberjacks, along with their families, had moved on to other locations. She knew she needed a high school education to be able to go to Bible school.

Esther's young mind told her that if she went to Prairie she could receive a good high school education and a Bible school degree at the same place. After carefully evaluating the different aspects of her future, Esther decided she was willing to leave the Caribou and pursue her goal of being a missionary. She told her parents, "I want to go to Prairie," and they started to make arrangements for her to attend Prairie High School.

Chapter 5

TO PRAIRIE HIGH SCHOOL

Near the end of August that year, Esther packed her suitcases and said goodbye to her friends and brothers. She got in the car with her mother and father and they started their two day drive through the mountains of British Columbia and western Alberta to the plains of central Alberta. The drive to Prairie was the beginning of a major change in Esther's lifestyle. She did not know it at the time, but never again would she live permanently with her mother and father. Her days of living in the forest and in a logging camp were finished. She would always be the little girl from the logging camp but never again live in one.

Even though her lifestyle was changing, the strong character and drive she developed from seeking adventure, facing dangers from wild animals and enduring the hardships of life in a logging camp would forever be with her. Esther's desire for adventure would be fulfilled as she obeyed the Lord's Great Commission to take the Gospel into the entire world. Little could she have imagined as they were driving towards Prairie High School that someday she would be in twenty-six different countries of the world.

Never did it enter her mind that she would be the pioneer of a great ministry to homeless children in a foreign country or that as a Canadian citizen she would someday be the president of a board of directors in a large ministry in America as they built a two million dollar building. Nor could she have imagined that someday she would see millions of dollars come in as support for other ministries in which she was involved.

She never dreamed that the decision to be a missionary, a decision she made when she was nine years old, would result in thousands of people's lives being blessed, both physically and spiritually. Yes, it could be said that the drive to Prairie that day was the beginning of a lifestyle change for Esther, but it really started back when she was nine years old and accepted Jesus as her Savior and said in her heart, "I want to be a missionary."

When they arrived at Prairie and drove into the campus, one of the first things they saw were the two sets of dorms, one on each side of the campus. Esther and her parents already knew about this because Prairie had sent them a map of the campus plus very detailed rules, requirements and guidelines that were required of every student. The rules stated that the boys' dorm was on one side of the campus and the girls' dorm on the other side. Never was a boy allowed to be on the girls' side, and a girl was not allowed to be on the boys' side unless they had prior permission. The rules also stated that if a student was caught on the other side, without proper permission, it would mean detention.

Actually, the students jokingly called the boys' sidewalk "blue" and the girls' "pink!" There was also a very strict dress code. A girl's hair had to cover her ears and be two inches below her neck or longer. They were not to wear makeup. Their dress was to be two inches below their knees, and their blouse or dress sleeves had to be at least half way to the elbow. Pants or jeans were forbidden, so skirts or dresses were worn at all times. The girls could wear small necklaces, watches, and a ring, but could not wear earrings. Esther and her parents agreed with these rules, so that was no problem for them.

As they drove slowly down the street towards the admissions office, they noticed that the place was very clean with freshly mowed green grass, nice shrubs and beautiful flower beds. The buildings were all plain, but very well kept. Standing in the center of the compound was a very large tabernacle that could hold several thousand people. Esther and her parents were very impressed with the appearance of the campus.

When they arrived at the admissions office, Fred parked the car and the three of them got out and walked in. The inside of the building was spotlessly clean, but very simple. There were several enclosed offices in the building, but they were very plain. The receptionist was a neatly dressed young lady in her early twenties wearing no makeup at all. Her hair was down to her shoulders and she was wearing a long sleeve blouse. Esther thought she probably was a Bible school student who was working at the school through the summer.

Fred introduced himself and told the receptionist that Esther was going to go to high school there. She was very friendly as she checked her records for Esther's name. It just took a few minutes and Esther was signed in as a new student. Then the receptionist told them where Esther's dorm was and what room she would be in. Esther already knew the name of her roommate because the two had been corresponding with each other.

After making the very short drive to the dorm, they got out and went in with Esther's luggage and found her room. The room was about eight feet wide and ten feet long with one window and a bunk bed. It was clean, but very plain with a rough board floor. There was a set of four shelves, two feet wide and four feet high, for each girl and one closet, four feet long, that they would share. The room also had a small table that both girls would be able to use for studying.

Esther already knew she would be sleeping on the top bunk because her roommate came earlier and chose the bottom bunk. After looking the room over for a short time, Esther and her mother made her bed, hung up her clothes and did a few other things to get Esther settled in. When they were finished, they walked back out to the car and Fred and Jenny gave Esther a hug, said goodbye, got back in their car and drove off. Esther watched their car drive down the street, turn onto the main highway and drive out of sight. She turned around and walked slowly back into her dorm and to her room feeling very lonely.

The small town of Three Hills was only three blocks away and the railroad station was four blocks away. That first night, when Esther was in her top bunk, she heard the train whistle at 8:25 P.M. and wished she were on the train going home – yes, she was homesick already. But of course she was too proud to let anyone know, so she just let the tears flow into her feather pillow, which her mother had made for her to bring to Prairie. Many times during the next two years, tears flowed into that pillow, especially when she heard the train's whistle!

Time passed quickly for Esther and soon she was able to adjust to her new surroundings and go on with her life at Prairie. The school required every student who stayed in the dorm to work on campus two hours every day to help pay for their living expense. They also required the students to write a letter to their parents every Sunday and bring it to the supper table; if they didn't have their letter, they could not have any supper that night. In addition to this, the students had to attend the required chapel services, go to their classes and do their homework. With all of this activity Esther had very little spare time, but she continued to hear the train whistle at 8:25 PM every evening.

Many times after she heard the whistle, she would think to herself, "I would like to be on that train and go back home." Occasionally she was able to go home for special holidays such as Christmas and summer breaks. During her summer breaks, she always got a job to help pay for her schooling. As a result, she spent very little time in the forest with her mother and father. This was hard for her, but she felt it was her responsibility to pay as much of her schooling cost as she could. During the summer after Esther graduated from high school, she got a job back in British Columbia in a city called Kamloops.

While Esther was in high school, her parents' logging business started to prosper and for the first time, they did not have to struggle to make ends meet. They had worked extremely hard, lived very simply for years to make it in the logging business and now things were going well for them. Shortly before Esther finished high school, Fred and Jenny purchased a large valley of several hundred acres of beautiful forest located between two mountain ranges. In the center of the property was a large lake called Dunn Lake. The property had a lovely log house on it located about fifty feet back from the water.

From their front window they had a beautiful view of the lake, the trees and the mountain range on the other side of the lake. There were also several smaller log cabins along the lake that they rented, mostly to fishermen and families from America. They called the place, "The Dude Ranch." It was in a remote area about a two-hour drive from Kamloops where Esther was working. People from America loved to come there and stay in a cabin for a few days to a few weeks, happy to pay for such a beautiful place. Many friends also came to stay in the cabins and even honeymooners who just happened to "find" each other at Prairie.

By this time Fred and Jenny also owned several logging operations in British Columbia. The one farthest north was just below the Yukon. Another logging business was near Cochrane, Alberta and they bought a home in Calgary so they could have a place to stay near that business. Managing their businesses kept Fred very busy and required that he and Jenny travel a lot between their two homes and the businesses.

Chapter 6
FIRST WOMAN TO DRIVE ROGERS PASS

About two weeks before Esther was to go back to Prairie for her first year of Bible school, another student from British Columbia who wanted to take two cars to Prairie, asked Esther if she would drive one of them for him and she agreed to do it. At that time a new road, called Rogers Pass, was under construction. When the new road was completed it would be only a one-day drive from Kamloops, British Columbia, where Esther was working, to Three Hills, Alberta, where Prairie Bible Institute was located. The old road called the Big Bend required a very hard two-day drive on a very rough, curvy road to get from Kamloops to Three Hills.

Esther dreaded to make the long drive over the Big Bend and started to think and pray about going over the Rogers Pass, even though it was still under construction and not open to the public. She knew a few construction trucks were making it all the way and she felt, with God's help, she could also make it. Esther was very confident of this, so she asked her father for his permission to do it. As strange as it might sound, Fred agreed with her. He knew Esther could do it.

Since Fred was a businessman, he knew people in high places in the British Columbia government. He knew the minister of highways who was in charge of the whole Rogers Pass project, so Fred went to him and asked for special permission to allow Esther to drive on the new road.

This was no small request, but because of who Fred was, the minister of highways thought about it for a while and agreed to give Esther a permit to cross on the Rogers Pass.

After packing her luggage and saying her goodbyes, Esther got in the car and headed east towards the Canadian Rocky Mountains. About two hours later she came to a small city in the mountains called Revelstoke where she filled her car up with gas. Esther drove on for a short distance and came to the western side of the new construction. She knew that for the next 100 miles she was going to have very rough driving. The people in charge knew she was coming, so they let her drive on to the unfinished road just like the big trucks were doing. There were bulldozers, earthmovers, large trucks and all kinds of large equipment working on the new road.

Her car seemed so small compared to the large earth moving equipment, but Esther kept moving even though it was very rough. At one point, she had to drive on two logs over a river. This was somewhat scary to her, but she started praying and slowly drove over them being very careful to keep her wheels right in the center of the logs. When she arrived safely on the other side, she said a special prayer thanking God for His help and protection.

Many times the unfinished road was very narrow and ran along the edge of a mountain with a thousand foot drop-off right at the edge. There were also many times when Esther had to drive through soft earth and sandy areas and at other times, on very rough rock filled areas. Along the way she was stopped several times where they were using explosives and blasting out areas that were solid rock. After about five hours of this type of driving, Esther came to the end of the construction and was back on a road that would take her to Calgary.

Later that evening, she arrived in Calgary, Alberta. Her mother and father were in their home in Calgary at that time, so Esther stayed overnight with them and the next day drove on to Prairie Bible Institute.

Esther was very thankful to God that she had made it safely and Fred was proud of his daughter's accomplishment. He knew she could do it. One of the local newspapers wrote an article telling the story of the first woman to drive across the Rogers Pass. It was little Esther. She made history that day!

Chapter 7
HER FATHER MURDERED

When Esther arrived at Prairie Bible Institute in 1961, she settled into her dorm and went to her first class on the fifth of September. She had matured a lot from the time she first went to Prairie for high school. She still missed her mother and father but was so dedicated to her studies and preparing herself to be a missionary that she hardly missed being at home. She loved her school and made many lifelong friends, both students and faculty. She especially loved the tabernacle services as they sang praises, worshiped and had Bible studies together. This was a great encouragement to Esther and it helped her grow in her desire to serve the Lord.

The school frequently had missionaries speak and tell about their experiences of serving the Lord in other countries. This caused Esther to be even more determined to be a missionary. While she was at Prairie she read Acts 1:8 many times and wanted to do exactly as it said.

Acts 1:8 But you will receive power when the Holy Spirit comes on you; and you will be my witnesses in Jerusalem, and in all Judea and Samaria, and to the ends of the earth. (NIV)

Many times after reading this verse, Esther's thoughts went back to when she was nine years old and had just accepted Jesus Christ as her Savior. Even though she did not know this verse back then, she still had a drive in her heart to be a witness for Jesus all over the world because of what He did for her. Esther wanted to make sure she took the right courses at Prairie to be a missionary, so she majored in Christian education and English and also took a minor in pastoral studies. This qualified her for missionary service and to be a youth pastor.

During Esther's senior year at Prairie she started to pray for God's direction for where she should serve Him as a missionary. She knew she could speak the Ukrainian language and wanted to go to Ukraine but the door was closed because of Communism. She continued to pray and ask God to lead her because she had no idea where He wanted her. One day as she was reading her Bible, she came to a verse that her eyes focused on in a way that she had never experienced before. She had a strong feeling that God was speaking to her as she was reading over and over 1 Thessalonians 5:24.

1 Thessalonians 5:24 The one who calls you is faithful, and he will do it. (NIV)

Esther felt the Lord was saying, "I am faithful. I have called you to be a witness for me in foreign lands and at home. I will do what is necessary for you to do this. Trust Me!" Esther had never experienced hearing from the Lord like this before. She could not explain it, but she knew He had given her this promise. Her part was to trust Him to bring it about. Esther took this as her lifetime verse.

Also during Esther's senior year at Prairie, she fell in love with another Bible school student named Bill (not his real name) and they were married one year after she graduated in 1965. Both Esther and her new husband planned to be missionaries, and they applied to be candidates at a mission called Worldwide Evangelization for Christ or WEC, as it is commonly called. They were accepted as candidates and went by train to the mission's headquarters in Fort Washington, Pennsylvania in August of 1966 to start their six-month candidate program on the first of September.

After the candidate program was finished, they were accepted as full time missionaries. They planned to go to South Africa and teach in one of WEC's Missionary Training Colleges (MTC), but before they went, they needed to get their prayer support by speaking in several churches.

WEC had the policy that their missionaries were not to ask for financial support. They believed if God called someone to go to the mission field any place in the world, He would provide their financial needs. They did not have to go around asking for support. WEC had almost 2,000 missionaries located in many countries and all were living by faith, believing God to provide for all of their needs. This had been their financial policy for over fifty years and their faith policy was working. God was supplying their needs without them asking for funds, but the mission did strongly believe that each missionary needed prayer support.

WEC missionaries were encouraged to ask churches and individuals to pray for them. Esther felt that it would not take long to get their prayer support and soon they would be missionaries in South Africa. She could not have been more elated. Her dream for the last sixteen years was being realized.

Little did she know, however, that within hours, she would receive devastating news. This would be the first of many heart-breaking events that would fall upon her within the next few years. Esther's belief that God could bring about His promise to her in 1 Thessalonians 5:24 was soon to be tested in a series of events, making it seem impossible for her to be a missionary.

It took a few days for Esther and Bill to make contacts and arrangements to speak in several churches. One morning the telephone rang at 6:00 AM in the mission dorm where they were staying. Esther immediately felt something was wrong because it was so unusual for someone to call at that time of the morning. The call was from Esther's mother-in-law. With Esther on one phone and Bill on the other, she told them that Esther's father was found dead from a gunshot wound! She knew no other details, but this news was so shocking that Esther could hardly comprehend what had happened.

Her mother-in-law was very gracious and sympathetic, but still her words were extremely painful to Esther. She was in such shock that she could hardly do anything but sob. Esther did not know she could hurt this badly because she had never experienced grief such as this. Sometimes she wondered if she were dreaming. Not only was Esther grieving because of her loss, but she was very concerned about how her mother was taking this.

After the initial shock, Esther and Bill knew they had to cancel all of their speaking engagements and go back to British Columbia. They did not have enough money for the flight, but the staff at WEC ordered their tickets anyway. A few hours later, a church in the area heard about their plight and gave them funds to pay for the tickets. Very quickly Esther and Bill packed their bags and were on a plane flying out of Philadelphia, Pennsylvania, at 6:00 PM. that very evening.

They arrived the next morning in Vancouver, British Columbia, where Esther's brother, Elmer was waiting for them. When she saw her brother standing in the terminal, she ran and hugged him and they cried on each other's shoulder. They went to have breakfast with a cousin who lived in the area and soon were on the four-hour drive through the mountains to Kamloops where Esther's mother was waiting. She was in extreme grief and still in so much shock that she could hardly talk to Esther and Bill when they arrived.

After they held each other and cried for a while, Esther asked one question, "Did Mike do it?" Esther's mother answered, "I think so." Then she relayed some details. Mike, one of Fred's employees, had not been seen since Fred had gone missing. Fred was supposed to meet with Mike and two business partners at one of the logging companies, but Fred and Mike did not show up for the 8:00 AM meeting in Kamloops. Fred had sold some of his shares in the company to these men, but he still owned the majority of the business. He had been ready to sell them the rest of his shares. These two men felt that it was not like Fred to miss a meeting and they were very concerned about him.

Fred did not come home to Dunn Lake the night before the meeting, but Jenny was not worried because they lived a long way from town, and sometimes he was not able to get home. One of the problems of getting there was crossing the North Thompson River by ferry, which was closed after 9 P.M. Since they did not have a telephone, she knew he couldn't call to tell her he would not be home.

The family had out-of-town guests and Jenny had to take them to the train station across the river in the morning, so she decided to drive into Kamloops and see if Fred was at the meeting with the men. When she got there, she asked if Fred had come for the meeting and they said he had not. Then she told them that he did not come home that night and they all became so concerned that they called the police.

No one knew where Fred was. The police thought he might have accidently lost control of his car and went over a cliff, so they searched all along the road from Dunn Lake to Kamloops. When they could not find the car, they decided to drag the river where the North and South Thompson meet in Kamloops. All this was to no avail.

Five days later, Fred's body was found in a very remote area. He had been shot once in the back and once in the head. They also looked for Fred's car for several weeks, but could not find it. Then someone saw a car parked in a strange area, checked it out and found it was his. They also found that Mike had purchased a gun and rented a car a few days before Fred came up missing.

As soon as she heard that her father was shot, Esther wondered if Mike had killed him. Jenny and the boys also wondered about this. About three years earlier, Fred's businesses became large enough that he decided to hire a full time accountant. Mike, a twenty-seven-year-old accountant, had the qualifications Fred needed, so he hired him. About two years later, Fred started to notice he had a lot less operating money than he should have. He did some checking into his finances and found he was missing several thousand dollars and then realized Mike had embezzled the funds.

Fred confronted Mike and showed him all of the evidence proving he had taken the money. He acted very sorry and confessed that he had stolen it. He begged Fred to forgive him saying, "If you do not prosecute me, I will pay it all back if you will let me continue working for you." Fred was a hard working businessman, but he also had a soft side and he forgave him with the understanding he would pay back the money. As a result Mike continued to be his accountant. Fred told Jenny about Mike's embezzlement and that he had forgiven him with the understanding he would pay it all back; however, Jenny continued to be very concerned about Mike's honesty.

Jenny told the two men who were at the meeting and the police about what had happened before with Mike and that she felt he probably was the one who killed Fred. They all agreed with her and started a manhunt for Mike. The police felt there was a chance he was hiding out in the forest and could decide to kill Jenny and her children. As a result, the police would not let Jenny go back to Dunn Lake to live until Mike was found and arrested.

They did let Esther, Bill, Ernie and Elmer go back and get a few things, but they were not to stay there overnight. They could only carry out a few clothes and personal items, but the house was still filled with very valuable and lovely family heirlooms, and they had no way to get them out.

Within a few days the probate court stopped all activity with the home, the bank and all of the businesses. The only money Jenny had was what she had with her when she drove into Kamloops to see if Fred was there. She only had a few clothes and personal items that her children carried out of her home in one trip. Some friends let her stay with them, but Jenny knew she had to find a place of her own very quickly. The problem was she had no money.

Three days after Bill and Esther arrived in Kamloops, two men came to the door to see Jenny. As Esther listened, the men told Jenny that Fred had a life insurance policy that had a paid up value of $5,000 even though he had not made payments on it for a long time. They handed her a $5,000 check. Jenny and Esther were very happy because it gave Jenny enough money for funeral expenses as well as some money for expenses while she was looking for a place to live and find a job.

As Jenny was thinking about Mike and what he probably did, she remembered he had come to the Dude Ranch by himself on the weekend before Fred was killed. It seemed strange to both Fred and her that he would have made the two-hour drive through the forest on the bad roads to visit them, but Mike told them that he "purchased" a new car (he actually rented it) and wanted to take both Fred and Jenny for a drive. This sounded very strange to Fred, and he told Mike they had company in the house at the time, and they were not going for a ride.

Mike also told Fred he wanted to talk to him about a sawmill that was for sale near Kamloops, so they could talk in the car. Once again, Fred said he was not going for a drive, but he could meet him in town the next day to see the mill. The next day was Easter Sunday and Fred was going to the Kamloops Hospital to pick up his nephew, so he promised to meet Mike before he went to the hospital.

Mike got back into his car and drove off. Fred was rather puzzled as to why Mike would drive all the way to Dunn Lake to take them for a car ride! Mike worked for him and they saw each other a lot, so this request just did not seem right. Now Jenny was wondering if Mike's intention was to kill both of them in case she knew something about the time he had embezzled the money. As Jenny thought about this, she felt the police needed to know this valuable piece of information.

After hearing this new information from Jenny, the police were very concerned about her safety and felt it was best if she and her family left the area for a short time. Jenny, Esther, Bill, Ernie and Elmer were staying with close family friends, but shortly after the funeral, they decided to do as the police advised. Ernie and Elmer went to the area where they had been living at the time of the death. Esther and Bill found a small house east of Lumby, B.C., which also provided a place for Jenny, and they rented it for three months. They hoped Mike would be found by then.

In July Jenny went back to Kamloops and rented a basement apartment that she could afford. It was a little damp and had high small windows, but it was a place where she could live. She also found a job at a laundry. It did not pay much, but it was a job. Jenny had some money left after the funeral was paid, so she was able to pay the rent on her apartment and buy some used furniture and a few other things she needed.

Jenny's life completely changed. She had been happily married, living in a very comfortable log house in a beautiful location. She also had sufficient money to buy the things she wanted. Now she was living by herself in a basement with almost no extra money and working in a laundry. The hardest part of it all was the fact that she was still in tremendous grief over the loss of her husband.

Often, she would think of her home on Dunn Lake, and how it was just sitting there with the doors padlocked by the probate court. She would love to go back and get some of her things, but she was not allowed to, even though she owned the place. She knew there was no heat in the house and that all of her clothes, furniture, and other things were getting very damp and possibly had mildew on them.

Esther was also grieving over the loss of her father and she hated to see her mother living like she was. She and Bill felt that they needed to stay in Kamloops and help her mother as much as they could. This meant she and Bill would not go to South Africa as they had planned. They helped Jenny get set up in her apartment and stayed with her until they could decide on their future.

The two businessmen who had shares in the logging company, started doing some investigating to see if Mike had embezzled more funds from the business. They found that he had and shortly before Fred was killed, Mike had sold nearly all of the sawmill equipment at the logging camp near the Yukon during spring break up.

Mike knew there would be no one there since the government does not allow logging trucks to drive on the roads in the spring because they become too soft when the ground thaws. Most logging companies totally shut down during this time, which could last up to two months. This gave Mike time to make some quick cash sales for the equipment. That camp was unable to resume the logging operation after the spring break up had finished because all the equipment was gone and so was the man who sold it along with the money he received.

The men had to tell Jenny there was hardly anything left of Fred's estate because Mike had taken nearly all of it. They could not tell exactly how much he had taken or how much, if any, was left. The final answer would come from the probate court after their investigation.

The police continued to look for Mike. About four months after Fred was shot, the police in Las Vegas, Nevada, received a phone call from a man who said, "I killed a man in Canada, and I came here and gambled all of his money away." The man then gave the police the name of the hotel and room number where he was staying. He also said, "I am going to kill myself and when you get here, I will be dead." The police rushed to the hotel, and by the time they got there, Mike had done just what he said he would do. They found him dead.

The police in Las Vegas found that Fred was the man Mike had killed in Canada. With a little more investigating, they found that the gun Mike killed himself with was also the one that killed Fred. There was no doubt that it was Mike who killed Fred. The police in Kamloops gave this information to Jenny. She was already sure of it, so it made little difference in her life, and it did not help to lessen the grief she was still experiencing.

After they found Fred's murderer and he was no longer a danger to Jenny, she began thinking about Esther and Bill and their desire to go to South Africa as missionaries. One day Jenny told them that she did not want this to keep them from going to South Africa. She said that she knew the Lord was going to take care of her and they should prepare to go to the mission field. Esther had been concerned about their future, and wondered what they should do; she knew that God had called them to Africa but she did not want to leave her mother, who not only lost her husband but whose life had changed so drastically. Esther was faced with a major decision. Was it best to stay in Kamloops and be with her Mother or should they go on to Africa? After much prayer Esther felt God was leading them to continue preparing for Africa. They would have to trust Him to take care of her Mother.

Satan tried to stop or divert Esther from following God's call upon her life. This happens to many who step out to live a life of obedience to the Lord. The way a Christian reacts to a painful situation makes a difference in how God will use them in the future. Esther could have become bitter and hateful because she and her mother had lost so much. Also, she could have blamed it all on God and stopped serving and obeying Him. Many Christians have done this after something terrible has happened in their lives. Almost everyone who has been greatly used of God has had a severe test in their life before He used them.

Even Christ Himself was tested before His ministry started. We see this in the fourth chapter of Matthew.

Matthew 4:1 Then Jesus was led by the Spirit into the wilderness to be tempted by the devil. (NIV)

Joseph was tested before God greatly used him.

Psalm 105:17-19 *¹⁷ and he sent a man before them—Joseph, sold as a slave. ¹⁸ They bruised his feet with shackles, his neck was put in irons, ¹⁹ till what he foretold came to pass, till the word of the LORD proved him true.* (NIV)

Abraham was tested before God greatly used him.

Genesis 22:1-2 Some time later God tested Abraham. He said to him, "Abraham!" "Here I am," he replied. ² Then God said, "Take your son, your only son, whom you love—Isaac—and go to the region of Moriah. Sacrifice him there as a burnt offering on a mountain I will show you." (NIV)

The Apostle James also talked about us being tested when we face trials.

James 1:2-3 Consider it pure joy, my brothers and sisters, whenever you face trials of many kinds, ³ because you know that the testing of your faith produces perseverance. (NIV)

Even though this test was bitter for Esther, it never entered her mind to stop serving the Lord. Her commitment to serve God as a missionary was still as strong in her heart as it was before her father was murdered. Esther passed her first test that Satan put on her and agreed with her mother that it was time for her and Bill to go on to Africa.

Esther did not know this at the time, but this was only the first test of many to come that Satan would throw into her path in order to stop her from serving the Lord.

Bill had a very old car that he had left with his parents when he and Esther took the train to WEC the first time. Within a few days after talking to Jenny, they had their car packed and were ready to make the 3,000-mile trip from British Columbia to their mission headquarters located on the north side of Philadelphia. Both Esther and her mother were crying as they hugged and said goodbye knowing it could be five years before they would see each other again. Esther and Bill looked very sad as they got into their car, waved goodbye to Jenny, and headed east out of Kamloops on their first leg of a trip to South Africa.

Chapter 8

TRAGEDY AND GOD'S BLESSING

After Esther and Bill arrived in South Africa they joined the missionary staff to teach at the Missionary Training College. Esther was finally working as a missionary and she loved it. She could not have been happier and believed this was where they would be ministering for years to come.

Esther did not know it but again Satan was going to throw a road block in her path in an attempt to stop her from serving the Lord.

About two years later, a problem arose and they were forced to close the Missionary Training College and return to America. Esther was very saddened and did not want to leave South Africa, but did not have any choice. Once again she was having to trust God for her future.

Esther and Bill went back to British Columbia and stayed there for a short time. Even though Esther and Bill's plans to serve God for years in South Africa did not work out, Esther determined that she was not going to stop serving the Lord in missions and they needed to continue in God's service in another area. Bill felt this way also and they returned to the WEC mission headquarters in Pennsylvania and helped in the ministry there. Esther worked in the kitchen and she loved it. She helped prepare meals for about forty-to-fifty people, including staff, candidates and many missionaries who were either on their way to the mission field or returning from different countries. Esther loved this ministry because she was still working with missions.

Esther's joy and happiness working at the mission headquarters lasted for about five years. Then Satan threw another tragedy into her life that took her out of mission work and left her as a single mother raising a ten-year-old son, Kevin and a seven-year-old daughter, Miriam. She was also left nearly penniless with a large house payment and other debts to pay. During this time, Esther was in extreme grief and cried nearly every day for weeks. She also felt it was impossible for her to ever again serve the Lord as a missionary.

Author's Note: I am purposely leaving out what the tragedy was. Many Christians can be left in tragic situations for many reasons. It can be a spouse's death, as it was in my case. At other times it can be divorce, the loss of a son or daughter, the loss of a job, loss of health, loss of finances, a home, a mother or father and many other things. During wartime, it can be a mate or child who was sent to the service or to war. If you are a Christian and living in a difficult situation and see no way out, please think of what you are going through as you read this book, and remember that God is faithful and He can do wonderful things for you, just as you will see what He did for Esther.

Esther went from being happy working in the Lord's service to being single with two children, in debt and over 3,000 miles away from her family in Canada. Looking over her bills, it quickly became evident that there was no way she could make the payments and have food for her children. Esther had been plunged into a financial mess and she saw no way out. She knew God was faithful and determined that she was going to trust Him to deliver her through the desperate situation she was facing. She went to prayer, sincerely asking God for His help in paying her bills and providing for her children. As Esther faced her financial situation she made three firm decisions. First, she would trust in God's faithfulness through it all. Second, she would always give back to the

Lord one tenth of any funds He gave her. Third, she would do all she could physically to make money to support her family and pay her bills.

After praying, Esther went to the bank where her mortgage was held and told them of her financial situation. She assured them that she would pay as much as she could on the loan each month, but said there might be times when she could not make the full payment. The bank official seemed to appreciate Esther coming to them, and he told her they would not foreclose on her house if she would pay something each month.

Then she had a very serious talk with Kevin and Miriam and told them they would have very little money and they could not buy anything extra. They were even going to have to be very careful when buying food. Both Kevin and Miriam agreed to help as much as they could, but they also said, "It is just not fair that we have to live like this." Esther answered and said, "Life is not always fair. If it gives you lemons, you make lemonade." This became a way of life for Esther's family. Life had given them lemons, and they had to make lemonade!

Esther saw that she had to work at more than one job, or she had to get a high paying job to pay her bills. She had an opportunity to take a job driving a large school bus in the morning and evening. Even though she had never driven a bus before, the school gave her some training and within a few days, she started driving. She found that she had time between her morning and evening shift of driving, so she looked for a job she could do during those hours.

She heard that a local plant nursery was looking for a secretary, so she went and asked if she could have the job and work from 9:00 AM to 3:00 PM. To her surprise, they agreed to hire her on those conditions. This gave Esther two jobs. She would drive the school bus in the morning, then go to the nursery to work from 9:00 AM till 3:00 PM, and immediately go back to her bus and drive it.

The two daytime jobs worked out well, but she still needed more money to pay her bills. Esther started to think about what else she could do in the evenings to make some more money. After checking around, she heard about the possibility of getting a job selling Tupperware in the evenings. This worked out fairly well because she was able to take Kevin and Miriam with her when she had a Tupperware party in people's homes. Then Esther thought about another way to make some money. She knew she was a good cook, so she started a business making wedding cakes on the weekends, and often she made birthday, graduation and other cakes.

Then another job of cleaning offices every Friday evening opened up and Esther took it. She knew this was a job her children could help her with and they could all make some money. During the summer Kevin mowed yards and gave some of the money to his mother to pay bills. The family also put out a half-acre garden to help provide their food. Even though Esther and the children were very busy, they always went to church on Sunday morning. She also had the policy that no matter how poor they were, she always paid her tithe to the church before she paid anything else.

Sometimes Esther got very tired working such long hours to make all the payments on the debts, the mortgage, utilities, food, etc. Even though she was working at so many different jobs, it was still very difficult to make the payments on all her bills. It had been also impossible for her to have any extra money and Christmas was coming. She was trusting the Lord, but there was no way she could buy any presents for Kevin and Miriam and have enough money to have a nice Christmas dinner. She just had to figure out a way, so she started praying and asking God to make a way for them to have a nice Christmas.

Then she remembered that some of Bill's building and carpet supplies were still in the old shed located on the back edge of the property. She went out and looked over the supplies. There were several five-gallon cans of unopened glue and paint plus a couple rolls of carpet and some other supplies. She thought there was a possibility of selling them, so she went to a man who owned a carpet store and asked if he would be willing to look at the supplies to see if he was interested in purchasing them.

The man came to Esther's house, looked the supplies over, and offered Esther $250 for them. Esther happily accepted his offer. Now she had enough money to buy some presents for her children's Christmas and enough to buy some special food for a Christmas dinner.

As Esther thought about buying presents for Kevin and Miriam, the Lord spoke to her in His still small voice and said, "Use the money to pay the bill at the hardware store where the supplies came from." Esther was not happy with what she heard, but she knew the Lord was speaking to her. She wanted to have the money for Christmas, but the Lord kept telling her to pay the bill at the hardware store. Finally, somewhat reluctantly, Esther took the money to the hardware store, went to the office and said she wanted to pay off the debt. The woman looked up the bill and it came to exactly the $250 that Esther had. Esther gave her the money and received a paid in full receipt.

The woman thanked Esther and she walked out not knowing what to do for Christmas. She did not know it, but another woman who worked in the store knew of Esther's financial situation and told the owner of the store. She said, "I know that woman. She hardly has any money, but she came in here and paid off the debt." The man was very impressed.

It was just two days before Christmas and Esther still had no money for presents. On that day she resigned herself to the fact that it would have to be a Christmas without presents. There was hardly any food because she did not have enough money. Later that evening there was a knock at the door. Esther opened it and there were several workers from the hardware store standing there holding Christmas packages and lots of food; there was special food that Esther would not have felt free to purchase even if she had some extra money. They said it was Christmas for Esther and her children from the hardware store and handed her a very nice Christmas card that all of the employees had signed.

There was also a letter in the envelope from the owner of the store. Tears came into Esther's eyes as she read it while the people were standing in her kitchen. He said, "I haven't known anyone to do what you did. I have watched many Christians' lives, but now I have experienced what Christianity is all about. You have shown us Christianity in action. Thank you." With tears flowing down her cheeks, Esther thanked the people for making it possible for her family to have a good Christmas. Some of them also had tears in their eyes as they wished Esther and her children a Merry Christmas and then walked out the door.

Esther eagerly went through the food to see what she had for Christmas and it was more than enough. There was no way she could have purchased that much even if she had kept the money. Then there were several presents for Kevin, Miriam and also for her. Esther thanked God over and over and also wrote the store a very nice thank you letter. It was the first Christmas Esther and the children had without Bill and God supplied and gave them a special Christmas. Esther saw God's faithfulness through it all and sincerely thanked Him for it.

Even though they had a very good Christmas, things continued to be very difficult financially. Esther struggled to pay her bills and have enough to buy food. After months of working at all the jobs, she started to feel exhausted. She also looked run down with dark rings under her eyes. Her weight dropped to around 100 pounds. She did not know how much longer she could continue working at the pace she was going.

She had wanted so much for God to use her in His work, but now there seemed to be no way it could ever happen again. She felt a lot like Job as in Chapter 19. He was innocent of doing any wrong and he didn't understand why things were going so much against him. Esther could not describe her pain to anyone in a way they could understand. She did not understand it either and had so many questions as to why all these things happened.

Author's Note: If Esther had been able to look ahead a few years, she would have seen that God was going to use her in a tremendous way in foreign countries and at home in America. Someday people would admire her for what God did through her and also for her drive and strength in doing His work. Many would even seek her advice as they were facing their own difficult situations. Blessings of hundreds of thousands of dollars would flow into the ministry in which the little girl from the logging camp was involved. She could not see how God was going to reverse the difficult time she was in at the time, but He was going to do it and would use her tremendously in His work in the future.

Esther had never experienced such exhaustion before. It became very difficult for her to continue working at the pace she was going. After a week of living in this exhausted state, she forced herself to start thinking about the fact that God did still love her and He was faithful. She was going to trust in His faithfulness no matter how tired she got. During this difficult time she still had a deep desire to be used of God in His service. After thinking about this, she opened the Word of God and asked Him to speak to her. She turned to Psalms 37 and as she began reading, verse four spoke to her heart. What an encouragement that was from the Lord.

Psalms 37:4 Take delight in the LORD, and he will give you the desires of your heart. (NIV)

Esther knew she had delighted herself in the Lord from the time she accepted Him as her Savior, and the desire of her heart was for Him to use her in His service. She felt He was saying that He loved her and He would continue to be with her as she faced the future. He would also give her the desire of her heart. Then Esther thought about the promise God had given her as she read 1 Thessalonians 5:24 during her senior year at Prairie.

1 Thessalonians 5:24 The one who calls you is faithful, and he will do it. (NIV)

She again determined in her mind that God was faithful and He was going to do what was necessary to bring about His call upon her life even though it looked impossible to her. These two verses encouraged Esther to move on and trust God for what He had for her in the future. This was a milestone in her life.

After only a few days, a woman came to her door with several bags of food, including milk. She told Esther that the Lord told her to buy these things and bring the food to her and the children. When Kevin saw the milk he spoke up and said, "Good, now we can have milk on our corn flakes rather than water." The woman seemed shocked and said, "I want to look in your refrigerator." Esther allowed her to look. When the woman opened the door she was shocked to see that it was empty!

Not long after this, Esther's financial situation came before the leaders of her church. They were informed about how Esther was working so hard to pay her bills and also how her children were helping. Possibly the woman who brought the food to her house told them what a hard time Esther was having financially. The church decided to pay one house payment to ease her burden.

Then the Sunday school class that Esther attended decided to take action and help her as well. They decided to assign a different family to Esther each month. That family would be responsible to make sure Esther and her children had what they needed for that month. This included maintenance on their house and appliances, plus their heat. They were also to include Esther and the children in on their family functions.

Some of the leaders in her Sunday school came and shared with Esther what they wanted to do. She was shocked and delighted. They were going to treat her like family! The class gave Esther a list of twelve families and the month each of them would be her family. They told her that if anything happened she was not to hesitate in calling her family that month for help. This was to start immediately. When Esther told Kevin and Miriam about it, they were very happy. There were also other families who did not go to Esther's church, but took them in like family. Esther started to see that Christians loved her and her children and that God had brought this about.

Right after the decision of the Sunday school class, Esther's bathroom and kitchen drain stopped working. She called her assigned family and within a short time, they were there to check the problem. They saw that a backhoe was needed to fix it and they took care of getting one there and the problem was fixed without any cost to Esther. Her assigned family took care of it all! Esther could not have paid for it, but God led the church to do it. Esther thanked God and the church for their love and help.

Each family invited Esther and her children to have meals with them often and took them out to eat. That was something Esther was not able to do, but God made it possible through their church. This family care continued and it was such a blessing to Esther. When winter came Esther had little money for heating fuel, so she turned her furnace down quite low. It was very cold in the house. Somehow her family found out about it and they had an oil tank truck come to her house and fill her tank. They paid for the oil and told Esther they would continue to pay for it, but she was never to let it get that cold in the house again.

Many other people helped Esther and her children as well. Every Friday, Esther would come home from work to find a $20.00 bill under her kitchen door. It was quite some time before she knew who put the money there. Then she found that it was an elderly gentleman who knew of her situation. What a godsend it was to her to have the extra money to help with expenses. In another case, a very dear friend from Canada sent a money order every month for a year. Another blessing was a wonderful, elderly couple paying for Kevin and Miriam to go to a Christian school. God provided for Esther and the children in many marvelous ways.

Life started to improve for Esther and the children. A large cosmetic company needed someone to work in the Human Resources Department writing and answering mail. This job went right along with Esther's qualifications, so she applied for the job and got it. She immediately started to make more money and liked the job very much. With the new job, Esther managed to find enough extra time to be very involved in a singles group in her church and she loved it very much.

Esther and the children continued to work hard and live very simply in an effort to pay off the bills, to make the house payments, and have enough money to live on. Esther still made wedding cakes and sold Tupperware and she had her half-acre of garden. After another four years, she had the bills paid off and had a little extra money to live on. One obligation remained. When Esther and Bill bought their house they borrowed $3,000 from Bill's sister to help with the down payment. She still wanted to pay the $3,000 back, but had not yet been able to do it.

Chapter 9

THE PROPOSAL

When Kevin was sixteen years old, news reached him that his friend Tanya McCauley had lost her mother to cancer. Tanya was living in Indiana with her dad and brothers Mike and Tony. They had become friends several years earlier when their families lived at WEC headquarters. He knew what it was like to lose a parent because he had lost his father years before. Mother's Day was coming, and Kevin could not help but think about Tanya not having a mother.

When Mother's Day arrived he asked his mother if he could call Tanya and tell her how sad he was that she lost her mother. He asked his mother to make the call and let him talk. Esther picked up the phone, and then she had a strange feeling that this call was going to change her life. She dialed the number and Tanya's father answered. She simply said, "Bob, this is Esther. Kevin would like to talk to Tanya." Bob said, "I will call her," and Tanya came on the phone. She and Kevin talked for about five minutes.

On Monday evening after Mother's Day, Esther received a phone call from Tanya's father, Bob. He asked Esther about her and Bill and wondered what was happening in their lives. Esther, Bill, Bob and his deceased wife, Pat, all knew each other from their time at WEC (Esther and Pat became friends and occasionally corresponded with each other). When Esther told Bob about the tragedy that happened and how she was now a single mother, he was shocked and very sympathetic towards

Esther for what she had gone through. He also asked how the children were doing through all this turmoil. Bob shared the details of Pat's cancer and passing away and the details of how his children were doing. An hour later, they both said goodbye and hung up.

On Friday evening of the same week, Esther received another phone call from Bob McCauley. When she answered the phone, Bob said, "Esther are you sitting down?" She said, "Yes, why should I be?" Bob said, "Knowing what I am going to tell you, yes, you should be." Esther answered, "What is it?" Bob replied, "Esther, I believe God has a future for you and me as husband and wife." Esther was completely shocked!

She hardly knew what to say and did not say anything for about a minute. Then she said, "What about love? I don't love you." Bob answered and said, "If God is in this He will give us love." Esther was uneasy with the direction of the conversation and wanted to end it as quickly as possible, so she said very little after that. It seemed to her that Bob sensed her uneasiness and did not pursue the conversation. Before he hung up, Bob did say, "I want to call you again," and Esther gave him permission to call.

The following week, Esther received a few phone calls from Bob. In one of them he said, "I want to drive out and see you." Esther answered Bob's request by saying, "No, I don't want you to come here, but if we are going to see each other, I am going to come there and see you. However, I don't have the money for a ticket, so you will have to buy it. I have a long weekend next week and that is the only time I can come."

Esther had taken time to think over Bob's proposal, but she was not sure it was the right thing for her to marry him. She also knew Bob had a very good job as a senior engineer with a very large company. If they did get married, Bob would not leave his job and come to Pennsylvania. She would have to go to Indiana to live and she wanted to see how he was living.

Bob answered right away and said he would buy a ticket the next day and send it to her by Federal Express. Within two days the ticket arrived, so Esther made plans to fly to Indiana on Memorial Day weekend. Esther was somewhat shocked when she saw the price of the ticket. It cost $500! She asked Bob why it was so expensive and he explained that he had a very hard time getting a ticket to Indianapolis on Memorial Day weekend because so many people were flying in to see the Indianapolis 500 mile race. When he finally found a ticket, it was very expensive, but he got it anyway. Esther knew the ticket had cost more than she could have saved in months, but Bob assured her it was worth it to have her come to see him.

Esther made arrangements for Kevin and Miriam to stay with her friends, Bob and Charlotte Smith, on the Memorial Day weekend. Early on Saturday morning, a friend drove her to the airport in Philadelphia and she got on a plane and flew to Indianapolis. During the flight she started to think, "What am I doing flying to Indiana to see a man I have not seen in years. I hardly know him, but here I am going to see him. This just seems crazy, but yet I am doing it."

As the plane was coming in for a landing, Esther had her first sight of Indianapolis. It looked to her much like any other city, but she was surprised to see the flat terrain. Soon the small plane touched down on the runway and she felt and heard the rumble of the tires rolling on the pavement. Then it taxied up to one of the terminals and stopped out on the tarmac. Esther got up along with all the other passengers and walked down the stairs, across the tarmac, and into the terminal. There stood Bob McCauley.

She recognized him right away and he also recognized her even though they had not seen each other in years. Esther looked Bob over and saw that he was neatly dressed in clean, casual clothes, clean-shaven and appeared to be a self-confident man. She had seen Bob before, but had paid little attention to him because he was always with his wife.

This time was different, however. He was looking at her in a special loving way that she appreciated. Bob immediately walked to her, put out his arms and gave her a hug. Then he told Esther how happy he was that she had come to see him and he welcomed her to Indiana. He suggested that since it was almost time for lunch he would take her to a restaurant where they could get something to eat and have time to talk.

As they were making the forty-minute drive to the restaurant, their conversation mainly centered on their lives for the last few years; however, Bob was anxious to tell her of something that happened when Kevin called to speak to Tanya. So, soon after they got to the restaurant and ordered their food, Bob told Esther that when she called and said, "Kevin wants to talk to Tanya," he handed the phone to her and walked to his bedroom. As he was walking through the doorway, the Holy Spirit came upon him so strongly that he fell on his knees at the foot of his bed. He prayed and said, "What is it Lord?" Bob went on to say that the Lord answered in His still small voice much like He did to Elijah, as found in 1 Kings 19:12-13.

1 Kings 19:12-13 ¹² And after the earthquake a fire; but the LORD was not in the fire: and after the fire a still small voice. ¹³ And it was so, when Elijah heard it, that he wrapped his face in his mantle, and went out, and stood in the entering in of the cave. And, behold, there came a voice unto him, and said, What doest thou here, Elijah? (KJV)

Bob said the Lord answered his question in the present tense and said, "That is your wife." Bob said, "I was shocked because it was like, in God's sight, you were already my wife. I wondered how this could ever be since you were married to Bill. It just did not add up. That is why I called you the next evening. After I heard about your tragedy and that you were a single mother, I realized we could get married." Then Bob said, "After we talked on Monday evening, the Lord spoke again and said in His still small voice, 'I want you to call her and propose, and I want you to let Me provide for her and her children through you.'"

Bob told Esther that it was very difficult for him to even think of calling and proposing. He continued and said, "I wanted to see you first." He went on to say that for the next four days he argued with the Lord saying, "I cannot do it without seeing her first." He said that at one time he told the Lord, "I want to see her first. I don't know this Esther. She might weigh 300 pounds and be meaner than a snake."

Bob said that by Friday evening he saw that the Lord wanted him to trust Him to pick out the right wife. He said he gave up arguing with the Lord and said to Him, "Lord, I don't know this Esther, but I do know You, and You have always been faithful to me, so I am going to call her right now and propose." Bob said, "Then I called you and proposed."

Esther was amazed at Bob's story, but was still not convinced it was God's will that they get married. As a result, she did not comment on what Bob told her. Bob did not pursue his story any further and their discussion turned to their present lives, rather than to the future. After they finished their lunch, Bob drove on for another forty minutes to his house. Esther was impressed when she saw it. It was a lovely three-bedroom ranch-style house in an upscale housing addition. It was very clean and even had a beautiful in-ground swimming pool in the back yard with a very nice concrete patio around it and a concrete fishpond with water lilies in it.

Esther had wanted to see how Bob was living, and she was well pleased with what she saw. His sixteen-year-old daughter, Tanya, was at home when they arrived. Esther had met her before, but she had not seen her for several years. The two of them seemed to hit it off very well. Later, Bob drove her to visit his two sons, Mike and Tony and their wives Michelle and Marcia. Esther was glad to meet Bob's sons again, and to meet their wives for the first time. They all had a good visit.

Esther enjoyed the day and that evening, Bob took her back to his home, where she stayed with Tanya, and Bob stayed with Tony and Marcia. As

Esther was lying in bed that evening, she thought about how impressed she was with the way Bob was living, but she was still not convinced it was right to marry him. It did make her feel good, however, that Bob was interested in marrying her.

Sunday morning Bob went back to his home to get Esther and Tanya for church. In the afternoon, his sons and their families came to his home, and they spent the rest of the day visiting. Bob and Esther did not talk further about the possibility of them getting married. Early the next morning, Bob took Esther back to the airport in Indianapolis, and she flew back to Philadelphia, PA. Bob asked Esther before she got on the plane if he could come and visit her, and she said he could.

The trip did nothing to convince Esther that she should marry Bob. She liked the way he lived and could see he made very good money. She knew she would no longer have to work if she married him, but she still was not convinced. She could see Bob was somewhat disappointed in the results of her visit, but she could also see he was not going to give up on marrying her because he knew it was God's will. She just had to leave it at that and see how things would go as she thought it over and prayed. The next day she got up as usual and went to her job, but now she had something special to think about, "Could it be that God had chosen Bob to support her and her children? Should she marry him?"

Two weeks later he called and told her that he wanted to drive to PA and spend the weekend with her. Esther told him it would be fine to come. She had some very close friends, Dave and Dottie Gehres, who had an extra bedroom where Bob could spend the night. It was 725 miles from Bob's house to Esther's home. Bob told Esther he would leave right after work at 5:00 PM Friday evening and drive all night, stopping a few times to get a few minutes of sleep and would probably arrive around 8:00 AM.

At about 8:00 Saturday morning, Bob arrived at Esther's house. The two had a very enjoyable day getting to know each other and visiting some of Esther's friends. Bob also visited with Esther's son Kevin. He and Bob had good fellowship talking about a car that Kevin was working on. Miriam was on a mission trip to France, so Bob did not see her. He stayed with the Gehres' that night and went to church with Esther and Kevin Sunday morning. After that, he made the 725-mile drive back to Kokomo, Indiana.

Bob continued to make the trip to see Esther almost every other week for the next six weeks and he also called her two or three times between his trips. During that time, Esther continued to pray about marrying Bob, but did not agree to do it because she was not sure it was God's will for her.

Kevin, however, was watching all that was happening and one day he asked his mother, "Did Uncle Bob ask you to marry him?" (When Esther's family lived at the mission headquarters, all of the children addressed the adults as either Aunt or Uncle, so he still called Bob "Uncle")

Esther was surprised by Kevin's question and she answered him with a simple, "Yes." Kevin replied, "If he did, then I think you would be foolish not to marry him. If you do, I am willing to move out there and finish my high school in Indiana." That was the end of the conversation and Kevin went on with what he was doing. Esther was left standing there with a new thought on her mind, "Kevin just gave me his approval for marrying Bob." She also thought about his statement that she would be foolish not to do so. She started to think about what he said and thought, "Could he be right?"

As the weeks passed, Esther did a lot of praying about marrying Bob and she evaluated it from every aspect she could. One of the things she thought about was how well he had treated his deceased wife. Esther knew Pat well and they had considered each other as very good friends. They not only corresponded with each other over the years, but spent time together as families when they were at WEC Headquarters. Esther saw Bob's love and concern for her. Esther remembered reading the McCauley's monthly missionary reports and she believed Bob was a very godly man and a godly father to his children. This gave Esther the impression that Bob would also treat her and her children in a godly way.

Most of Esther's friends met Bob and encouraged her to marry him, but she needed to hear from the Lord. What was God saying to her? As the days and weeks passed, knowing God's will became her greatest goal and she spent a lot of time daily praying for God's direction. Then it happened. She could not explain it, but she knew it was God's will for them to be husband and wife.

This happened during the last week of July 1985. Esther said to herself, "I will marry Bob and do it right away because I believe it is God's will. If I wait until my children are out of school they will never think of Indiana as being their home and they will not want to come there. If I do it this summer, they will finish their school there and that will be their home. I will tell Bob right away and make plans to marry him this August. I still don't love him, but I know it is God's will for me." Bob came the following weekend and Esther told him she knew it was God's will for her to marry him and they should do it in August. Bob was very pleased about her decision and they immediately started to make plans for their marriage.

Esther told her friends about her plan to get married in August and said she was going to have a very simple, only family, wedding. They all were very happy for her, but several of them wanted her to have a wedding that included her friends!! Esther said, "I don't have time to make all of the arrangements for a big wedding because I have to get so many things done in my home to be ready to move to Indiana in two weeks." Esther's friends asked if she would mind if they planned the wedding, and of course, she was happy to have them take over. One friend made lovely wedding invitations and sent them out. Another offered her beautiful backyard for the wedding.

Esther loved this idea. She had two other friends who were very musical; one played the organ and the other played the piano. Both volunteered to play and took care of the details of getting a piano and organ in the backyard for the wedding. Another took care of getting the flowers and someone else took care of arranging for the chairs. A dear and close friend made a beautiful wedding cake as her gift to Bob and Esther. A festive brunch was made with several friends bringing food. Esther's friends took care of every detail. Bob and Esther both wanted a missionary friend, Dwayne Olson, to marry them and he agreed to perform the ceremony. Bob's children and grandchildren all came to Pennsylvania for the marriage, as well as Bob's nephew and wife.

Chapter 10

A NEW BEGINNING

So it was, on August 17, 1985, Bob and Esther were married in a very beautiful outdoor wedding with about 100 friends present. Standing with them were Esther's children, Kevin and Miriam and Bob's children, Mike, Tony and Tanya, as well as grandson Andrew, as ring bearer, and granddaughter, Katrina as flower girl. When Dwayne Olson pronounced Bob and Esther husband and wife, it was a very special moment for both of them. It was a beautiful wedding with many friends witnessing what God had done!

They both knew God had brought about the circumstances that brought them together and that He wanted them married. Esther knew that what had taken place to bring her and Bob together was proof that God loved her so much that He gave her a man who would love and care for her and also be a godly father to her children. Bob knew God loved him so much that He gave him a godly woman who would be a helpmate to him and present a godly mother image to his children and grandchildren.

That day was especially significant for all who were there. Bob's children told him a few months before that they felt it was time for him to find a good woman and get married. Mike, Tony, and Tanya knew they had just witnessed their desires for their father fulfilled and they were happy about it. Esther's son Kevin was especially happy. Esther's friends had watched her go through some very difficult times and now they saw the promise of happiness for her. They also remembered how hard she worked to pay her debts and they knew she would no longer have to work like that, because Bob was able to support her and the children.

Another great thing had happened that no one, including Bob or Esther, knew about. It was the beginning of a very prosperous life for Esther to serve the Lord in a way that would touch the lives of thousands of people for Jesus Christ.

Bob and Esther went to the Pocono Mountains for their honeymoon and had a lovely time. Then they returned to Esther's home and loaded her family's belongings into a U-Haul trailer to take back to Indiana. Also, during that time, a young couple from Esther's church rented her house. Three days later, Esther and Bob started on the long drive to Indiana. Bob's son, Mike, had loaned him his truck for the trip, because they had to pull the U-Haul trailer. Earlier, Esther's friend, Charlotte Smith, drove Esther's car and took Kevin and Miriam to Bob's home in Indiana. She waited until they arrived, and then she flew back to Pennsylvania.

It didn't take long for Esther to settle into her new home. Kevin had his own room, and Miriam and Tanya shared a bedroom. The big attraction for all three of them was the swimming pool; the children got along great from the very beginning and the day after Bob and Esther arrived, they started their first day in school. Kevin was excited because the school had an auto mechanics class.

During their drive back to Indiana, Esther started to have a serious physical problem. Bob became very concerned about it and phoned ahead to his doctor for an appointment for her the day after they arrived. After the doctor examined Esther, he said she had a tumor that needed to be removed right away. Two days later she was in the hospital having surgery. Bob had lost his first wife with cancer and he was very concerned that Esther's tumor might be malignant. As soon as the surgery was over, the surgeon told Bob that the tumor was not cancerous and they had successfully removed it. Bob was extremely thankful when he heard the good news.

While Esther was recovering from her operation, she was invited to join a local Bible study, which proved to be a real blessing. This study gave Esther the opportunity to meet people in her new community and to feel at home in Indiana. One day during the Bible study, Esther shared with them the tragedy she had been through. She also gave details of how she could see no way out of her financial situation and how God was so faithful and helped her get through that difficult time. Some women in the area, who had heard about how God brought Esther through this low time in her life, wanted her to mentor them because they were is a similar situation.

Also, some of the pastors in the area told women, who were going through a very difficult time, that it would be good for them to talk to Esther McCauley. These pastors felt Esther would understand what the women were going through and she could help them because she had gone through the same thing. Esther seldom advised the women do anything specific in their situation, except to make things right with God through His Son Jesus Christ first, and then let Him work things out for them as He had for her.

Most of the women did not expect Esther to have a special direction for them, but rather she was someone they could talk to who understood their circumstances. Even some younger women who didn't have problems, asked Esther to mentor them. She had not sought after this ministry, but it seemed to both her and Bob that God was using her to help many others with what she learned during her difficult time.

Bob took Esther to visit his friends, aunts and uncles, cousins and other extended members of his family and they all accepted her with open arms. Some of them even called Bob after they met her and told him how much they liked Esther. These comments made her feel like she was a part of his family.

Prior to her marriage to Bob, Esther had not seen her mother in two years and had not seen her brothers in almost four years. She had not been able to attend any of her grandparents' funerals, family weddings or even family reunions, because she could not afford the trips.

Esther told Bob how hard it was for her to miss all these family functions. After hearing her sentiments, Bob promised her that he would make sure she could go to western Canada at least once a year to see her family and he would make sure she got to go to her family events. Not long after they were married, Bob and Esther went to British Columbia and Esther was able to visit her mother, stepfather, brothers, and many of her aunts, uncles and cousins. The trip helped Esther renew family relationships and made her feel like she was part of her family again.

About a year after Bob and Esther were married, they were asked to be Midwest representatives for WEC. This meant they would be speaking in churches and Bible colleges representing WEC. Bob and his first wife, Pat, did this before she became ill and passed away. Now they were asking Bob and Esther to fill this position.

They knew Esther had knowledge of WEC and their policies, so she would be a good representative for the mission. Since Bob was working, he could not always go to the mission conferences at Bible schools or colleges, so Esther went by herself. Sometimes she was gone for several days at a time speaking and teaching on missions. Bob always encouraged and helped her in any way he could in this ministry.

Esther loved being involved with the mission again, and she was thankful for the opportunity. When she was going through her financial struggles as a single parent, she thought it was impossible for her to ever be in missionary service again, so this was a special blessing. Esther was very busy in the Lord's work, but she also had time for her family because she did not have to be constantly working to pay her bills. Bob continued to work in engineering and was doing very well on his job. As time went on, he also received some very substantial raises in pay, which helped greatly in their finances.

The young couple who were renting Esther's house decided to move out after they had been there only a short time. At that time, Bob and Esther decided to try and sell the house. Esther had tried to sell it before they were married, at the same price she and Bill paid for it, but no one was interested in it. She had a very close friend who was a realtor, so they decided to let her sell the house. Since she was Esther's friend, she knew the house well and suggested they put it for sale at a very high price. Esther reminded her that they had tried to sell the house before at a very low price and were unable to sell it, but her friend still felt they should ask a high price for it, so Esther and Bob agreed.

Exactly three weeks after they put the house on the market, it was sold at just under the asking price. Esther and Bob were amazed, but very happy because this gave them some extra money. The first thing they decided to do with the money was to pay Bill's sister and her husband the $3,000 that Bill and Esther had borrowed from them. Next, they decided to pay a hospital bill that Bob still owed for Pat's treatment before she passed away. After paying those bills, Bob and Esther still had money that remained in the bank for future use.

Bob was also making more money from his engineering job than they were spending, so their bank account was growing monthly. They realized that God was prospering them financially, and they thanked Him for it. Esther was extremely happy about this because she had worked as hard as she could for a long time and made just enough money to live on and pay off the debts. Now things were different. She did not have to work outside her home and, for the first time in her life, was able to save some money.

Chapter 11
A NEW HOUSE

Bob & Esther had been married two years when they received an important phone call from one of their friends. She told them that her daughter and husband had a waterfront property on the Kokomo Reservoir that was for sale and she wondered if they would be interested in buying it. The price they were asking sounded very reasonable. Bob and Esther knew that a waterfront lot in their area would sell very quickly if the price was right, so they immediately drove out to see it.

They would have to build a house there, but they knew they could do it. Right away, they called the owners of the lot and offered to purchase it. Within a week, all the papers were signed and the land belonged to Bob and Esther. They were both delighted with their purchase and thanked God for the beautiful property He had given them. Immediately, they put their house up for sale because they needed the money from it to build their new home. They planned on moving into an apartment after they sold their house and then they would start building their new home.

At that time a recession was going on in America, and property was not selling well because the interest rates were about sixteen percent. Several people looked at Bob & Esther's home and wanted to buy it, but could not afford the mortgage payments. One day three women, along with the realtor, came to look at the house when Esther was there. As they were walking around, they started to speak to each other in a foreign language. As they were speaking, Esther was talking to the realtor, but she could hear the women.

They were speaking Ukrainian! Esther understood almost every word they were saying. One woman was complaining about several things. She did not like the color of the paint, the layout of the rooms, the cabinets, etc. Esther knew the house was spotless when they came, so she did not complain about that, but she complained about almost everything else. Finally, the three women spoke to the realtor in English and told her that they were ready to go.

Then Esther spoke to them in Ukrainian and thanked them for coming. The women were visibly shaken up as they realized Esther had understood the woman's complaints. Esther carried on a small conversation with the women before they left. All of them, including the realtor, found it interesting that the four women all spoke a language from a very far away country and they were all living in Indiana.

A few months later, a young couple looked at the house and made an offer with the condition they could have possession in one week. The man had just gotten a job with the company where Bob worked and they wanted to move from another state to Indiana right away. They had already been pre-approved for a loan, so they could have the money to pay for the house right away. Bob and Esther accepted their offer, and the sale was finalized three days later. Within the week, they moved out of their house into an apartment and also left their home spotlessly clean for the young couple to move into.

By this time, both Kevin and Tanya were married and moved into their own homes. Bob had spent a lot of time designing a nearly 3,000 square foot house that looked very much like a Swiss Chalet. It had nearly 2,000 square feet of living space on the first floor and about 1,000 on the second. The second story was to be used as a place where traveling missionaries could stay, either overnight or longer, for a time of rest.

Bob and Esther decided to call the second story their missionary guest area. It would have a thirty-foot-long living room with a kitchen in one end that missionaries could use if they wanted to do their own cooking. One wall would have four large windows overlooking the water, so they could enjoy the view. There would also be a master bedroom and a smaller one with a bathroom between them. Bob and Esther wanted their guest area to be a blessing to every missionary who stayed there.

As Bob was designing the house, he constantly asked Esther for her input, and Esther loved giving it. If she wanted something changed, Bob did what he could to meet her desires. Esther never dreamed she would have a beautiful home like he was designing and she praised God for His goodness to her.

Shortly after Bob and Esther sold their home, they had their design finished and started making plans to build on their new lot. Bob contracted someone to put in the foundation and then contracted a man to rough frame the house and another one to put on the roofing. From there Bob and Esther did nearly all the work themselves to finish the house. Bob was at his job for about nine hours a day, and then he would spend another eight hours building the house. During the days and on into the evenings, Esther did all she could to help.

Within six months, the second floor of the house was completely finished, and they moved into that part of the house. It was so refreshing for them to be living in their new home even though the first floor was not finished. Esther loved it even more than she thought she would. Almost daily, she looked back at the time in her life when she was working long hours to pay her bills and buy food for her family, and she would thank God for how He was blessing her.

After they moved into the upstairs of their house, Bob and Esther worked together nearly every day finishing the first floor. They were doing all of the work themselves, so they would not have to borrow even one cent to finish their house. As time went on, God blessed, and they were able to completely finish their home. They owned a new and quite large home on a waterfront lot, and it was completely paid for. It was like God was opening the floodgates from Heaven and pouring out a blessing upon them according to Malachi 3:10.

Malachi 3:10 Bring the whole tithe into the storehouse, that there may be food in my house. Test me in this," says the LORD Almighty, "and see if I will not throw open the floodgates of heaven and pour out so much blessing that there will not be room enough to store it. (NIV)

When Esther was alone and struggling to meet her financial obligations, the first thing that came out of her paycheck was her tithe. She knew that God would bless and supply her needs. Now, neither Esther nor Bob could deny that God was pouring out a blessing upon their finances. They were continually amazed at how they were able to buy things so cheaply.

They were able to put in their whole heating system including the heat ducts and furnace for only $250. Their entire water system including the pump, wiring, regulator and tank only cost them $110. After it was finished, everyone who came to Bob and Esther's home were amazed at how beautiful it was, and when they found out that they did not have to go into debt to build it, they were even more amazed.

Bob and Esther wanted to put in a boat dock in front of their house but knew it would cost a few thousand dollars to purchase a large professionally built floating dock with a steel frame and catwalk that would not rust. Then one day, when Bob was at work, a friend told him that a sales representative came in and said he had a very high quality boat dock that he would give to anyone who would just take it out of the water and move it.

Bob took him up on the offer right away and got a few of his friends along with his son Kevin, and they moved the dock and put it in front of Bob and Esther's lot where it is still to this day. The dock was of even better quality and size than Bob had thought about getting and they knew it was God who gave it to them at no cost.

Shortly after Bob and Esther moved into their house, they contacted WEC, New Tribes Mission and Wycliff Bible Translators and volunteered their home for traveling missionaries to come and stay overnight or longer, if needed. They could have three meals a day with Bob and Esther at no cost or could cook for themselves. From that time on, they were blessed to have missionaries from all across the world spending time with them.

Chapter 12

THEIR DAUGHTER'S ACCIDENT

About two weeks after Bob, Esther, and Miriam, moved into their new house, Miriam drove into town to run a few errands for her mother. She had been driving for about a year and was driving her own car that evening. Esther started preparing dinner shortly after Miriam left and was expecting her home any minute when the phone rang. She picked it up and said, "This is Esther." Bob was sitting at the table when he suddenly saw a very concerned look on her face. Then he heard her say, "Which hospital is she in?" Esther responded quickly, saying, "We will be there as soon as we can." Then she hung up the phone and said, "Oh Bob, Miriam has been in a serious accident! They said she is hurt badly and we need to get there right away!" Very quickly they ran to the car and headed for the hospital in Kokomo. As they were driving, Bob tried to prepare Esther for the possibility that Miriam was in critical condition.

The drive only took about ten minutes and they walked into the emergency area and to the front desk. The receptionist was expecting them and a nurse quickly led them to a room and said, "Your daughter is in here." Bob and Esther walked in and saw Miriam lying on a table. Miriam's face was cut up so badly that they could barely recognize her. Both Bob and Esther almost went into shock as they looked at what was once their beautiful daughter. She was tightly strapped to a wooden stretcher and her head was held on the stretcher in such a way as to make it impossible for her to move it. She was also unconscious and not moving. The hospital had already taken x-rays, showing that her neck and back were fractured. When Bob & Esther heard the news, they realized that Miriam might be paralyzed for life, and even the thought was almost more than they could bear. Then a nurse came in and said, "We need to lifeline her to a hospital in Indianapolis right away."

A young police officer came to them and explained what had happened. A semi-truck and trailer had made a left hand turn across oncoming traffic, causing Miriam and another driver to hit it broadside. Miriam's car went completely under the trailer which cut the top completely off. She was not wearing her seat belt, and the impact threw her under the dash before the trailer frame cut off the top of her car. If she had been wearing her seat belt, she would have been decapitated. The other driver hit the cab of the truck and ruptured the fuel tanks. He was injured, but not nearly as seriously as Miriam.

The nurse asked Bob to go to the nurse's desk while Esther stayed with Miriam. The woman behind the desk explained to Bob that they needed him to sign some permission and financial responsibility forms. Bob knew the cost could be a hundred thousand dollars or more, but he gladly signed the forms and gave his permission to take full financial responsibility for the cost to lifeline Miriam to Indianapolis and to operate on her as needed. After signing the forms, Bob went back into the room where Esther and Miriam were.

Only a few minutes later, they rolled Miriam out to be flown to Indianapolis. Bob and Esther drove directly to the hospital and went immediately to the emergency ward. By the time they got there, Miriam was already in the operating room. The operation took five hours. During this time, Bob and Esther were praying as they sat in the waiting room. They did not know until later that there were three surgeons operating on Miriam. When the operation was over, one of them told

Bob and Esther that Miriam's neck was fractured in one place and her back was fractured in two places.

The main issue they were concerned about was the possibility that her spinal cord was damaged and this could cause her to be partially or fully paralyzed. Then he told Bob and Esther about her face. She had two massive cuts on her face that would leave scars. In addition to that, she had multiple small cuts on her face, and a lot of glass was imbedded deep in her face, which the doctors were unable to get out. They said it would eventually work its way out, but it would take a year or two. He also said she was partially scalped, and they did what they could to repair that, but she would have a place on the top of her head where her hair would never grow again.

After the surgeon left, Bob and Esther sat there dazed as they wondered what Miriam's future would be. They realized that she could be paralyzed. They had hoped the doctor would tell them that she was going to be okay, but he didn't tell them anything encouraging. They also knew the surgeons had done all they could to help Miriam. They both realized that the only answer to this terrible tragedy was prayer for God to heal her.

That night Bob and Esther did a lot of praying and very little sleeping. The next day, they asked many churches and individual Christians to pray for Miriam. A few days later, when she was fully conscious, the doctors gave her some tests to see if she could move her feet, legs, arms and hands. She passed the tests, and the doctors said she would be able to walk again. Miriam was not told that she might not be able to walk, so she just took this in stride as if it were routine.

On the other hand, Bob and Esther were thanking God and rejoicing because Miriam was going to be able to walk again. For the next few weeks, they spent nearly every night sleeping on chairs in the hospital, so they could be with her. Even when Bob had to work during the day, he drove to the hospital every evening.

Miriam was put on a wooden stretcher when they took her out of her wrecked car and they did not take her off that stretcher for two weeks. Even during the operation, they left her on it. Finally, it was time to take her off the stretcher and put her in a Minerva Brace that held her back and head so tight she could not move them at all, and she could not even open her mouth. The medical staff taught Miriam how to hold a straw tightly between her lips and to suck liquid nourishment between her teeth. After Miriam had recovered enough to do this, the medical staff brought in a schoolteacher who worked with Miriam in an effort to get her caught up on the schooling she had missed.

After three weeks in the hospital, Miriam was released to go home, but she had to remain in the Minerva Brace for two more months. It was near the end of April 1989 when the nurses carefully helped her get into the back of Bob and Esther's car. It was a happy day for all three of them, but a very painful one for Miriam. Bob tried to miss all of the bumps he could and to drive slowly, but even the smallest bumps gave her some pain.

After an hour of driving, they arrived at their new home, and they carefully helped Miriam to her bedroom where she would spend a lot of time for the next two months. The hospital wanted a nurse to check her out regularly during the next two months. Esther asked Karen Long, a family friend, if she would be that nurse and she gladly agreed to help.

When Miriam came home, her hair was matted with dried blood and some remaining slivers of glass especially under the Minerva Brace that covered most of the back of her head. After a few days, the dried blood started to smell quite bad. Miriam did not know it, but her whole room smelled bad. With Karen in the lead and Esther helping, they carefully put Miriam face down on a plastic sheet on her bed, removed the back of the Minerva Brace and washed and combed her hair until it was perfectly clean. Then Karen carefully re-mounted the Minerva Brace. They opened the windows to let some fresh air in and soon the foul odor was gone. Miriam felt much better after this because her hair was clean, and most of the glass was removed.

A few days after Miriam came home, one of her high school teachers came to visit her and talk to Esther and Bob. Miriam's accident happened near the end of her senior year of high school and she would not be able to go back to school before the end of the year. Bob and Esther, and also Miriam, thought she would probably have to re-take her senior year in order to graduate. The teacher encouraged them that it was still possible for Miriam to graduate. She said if Miriam would study at home and the school got someone to mentor her, she could catch up to her class. Miriam would have to take all the exams and pass them, but it could be done, especially with a mentor.

Esther, Bob, and Miriam were delighted with this possibility and were so thankful for the help the school was willing to give to make it all happen. For the next few weeks, Miriam worked hard even though she was in her bed a lot of the time and the school mentor did a wonderful job. This made it possible for her to finish her courses and pass her exams. By the graduation date, Miriam could walk very slowly even though she was still wearing her Minerva Brace.

Esther and Bob took her to the graduation, and she was able to put on her cap and gown over the brace. It was very obvious that she was wearing the brace, but when her name was read to come forward to get her diploma, she very slowly walked towards the principal to get it. When she was about twenty feet from him, her whole class stood up and gave her a standing ovation. Esther and Bob both started to weep as they witnessed the respect the students gave Miriam for her accomplishment, in spite of her very difficult time.

Miriam continued to improve, and a month after she graduated, a nurse at the hospital in Indianapolis removed her Minerva Brace. The nurse had her make some movements to see if her neck and back were healed well enough to leave the brace off and everything appeared fine.

She was able to go home and eat solid food for the first time in two months. Taking her food through a straw had been very difficult, so it was refreshing for her to be able to eat solid food.

Slowly she got her strength back and was able to carry on normally. She learned how to use makeup to cover the two scars on her face and to comb her hair in such a way as to cover up the place on top of her head where her hair would not grow. Miriam looked beautiful again and was married two years later. Esther and Bob thanked God over and over that she was not killed and that she could walk and have a normal life.

Chapter 13
AID TO CHRISTIANS IN MOSCOW

In August of 1991, Esther read an article in the local newspaper about a young Russian man from Moscow named Yuriy who was working as an exchange engineer in the company where Bob worked. In the article, Yuriy described the situation in Russia as very unsettled and life was difficult for his family because everything was very expensive. He said it took two months of his Russian wages to buy a snowsuit for his two-year-old son and eight hours wages to buy one aspirin. When Esther read the article, she was very touched and wanted to do something to help Yuriy's wife and little boy. She had vivid memories of how difficult it was for her when she was trying to raise her children and hardly had enough money to feed them.

Life was different now because God had blessed her and she had enough to reach out and help others in need. Esther thought about how she could help and decided she could get a snowsuit and a few other items, put them in a box and send them to Yuriy's family. She was excited about the idea and picked up the phone to talk to Bob while he was at work. He was at his desk at the time and answered right away. Esther told him about the article and asked if it was okay with him if she sent a few items to Yuriy's wife in Moscow. As Bob was listening to Esther give him the details about the article, he was also praying and asking God to direct him in his answer. Bob felt the Lord was saying, in His still small voice, that he should tell Esther to do it.

With Bob's support, Esther found out how to reach Yuriy and phoned him at work to tell him what she wanted to do. Yuriy expressed his appreciation for her generosity and he told her there was another woman in Kokomo named Barbara Brown who called him and wanted to do the same thing. He suggested that the two women get together and work out what they would send.

Esther did not know Barbara, but when she called her and told her what she wanted to do, Barbara said to Esther, "I think I have heard about you. Don't you have a Bible study in your home?" After Esther replied that she did, Barbara said she and her husband Ed were Christians and they both wanted to help. Then she invited Esther and Bob to come to their house for Sunday dinner, and they would discuss what they were going to do. Barbara also invited Yuriy.

The following Sunday, Esther and Bob went to the Brown's home and met Ed and Barbara, as well as Yuriy. Barbara had prepared a lovely meal, and after enjoying fellowship together, they discussed plans for the Browns and the McCauleys to send a few boxes of clothing and other items to Yuriy's wife and son.

During Esther's Tuesday Bible study that week she told the ladies what she was planning to do to help the young Russian's wife and little boy. She told them that she was planning to send two or three outfits of clothing for the little boy as well as some clothes for Yuriy's wife. A few of the women had little boys and they offered to give Esther some of their clothes, which were used, but in good shape. Others said that they had clothes of their own that they would like to give for Yuri's wife. Esther agreed and felt she could pick out enough outfits of clothes to fill one or two boxes and send them to Yuri's wife. The ladies really got excited about this project and they wanted to send more than just two or three boxes of clothes to the family. Right away, they started to go to yard and garage sales and within a few days, they brought so many clothes to Esther that it nearly filled their two-car garage. However, no one had thought about the cost to send the clothes to Russia!

When Bob came home from work and saw their garage full of the items for Russia, he told Esther that he estimated it would cost a $1,000 or more to send them and maybe they should stop collecting. Word traveled fast that the McCauleys and the Browns were sending clothing to Russia and within a couple of days, so much was donated that Bob and Esther's garage could not contain it all. The McCauleys talked to the Browns about this problem and Ed suggested they move to a large unused room where he worked. More and more people brought donations and very soon that room was filled!

This all happened within a few days and it became almost out of control for both the McCauleys and the Browns. People from all over the area were bringing very nice clothes to send to Russia. Esther and Bob and the Browns began wondering if God had brought this all about to do something much greater than just sending a few clothes to the one family in Russia. After praying about that possibility, they believed God was leading them to send a forty-foot-long overseas shipping container of clothes, food and medical supplies to Russia. This possibility became a reality in the minds of both families, and they completely changed their goal of sending a few clothes to Yuriy's family to sending clothes and supplies to Moscow as humanitarian aid for many families.

Soon after the large room where Ed worked was filled with clothes, a building contractor volunteered to let them use a very large area in one of his heated warehouses. They moved again, to the new location, and it was so large they knew they would not run out of space.

The newspaper that published the article about Yuriy found out about the McCauley and Brown's plan to send humanitarian aid to Russia, so they sent a reporter to the warehouse to interview Esther and Barbara. He wrote another article about their plan to send supplies to Russia. When that story came out, more items were donated for Russia, ranging from food and medicine to clothing for children and adults. It seemed like everyone in the county wanted to help. A local dry cleaner offered to clean coats and jackets free of charge and the women from a Mennonite church brought sewing machines and mended many pieces of clothing. Others took clothes home and washed them. Both the Browns and the McCauleys wanted to ship only clothes that they themselves would wear. This became their guideline for accepting clothes for Russia.

The Browns and McCauleys began checking on requirements for sending an overseas container and found that every box had to be numbered and an inventory made listing the items in each box. Each box number and its contents had to be put on the shipping manifesto. Before the shipment could leave America, inspectors would pull different boxes from the container and examine them to see if the contents were exactly as listed on the manifesto. If they were not, the shipment could not be sent. The McCauleys and the Browns recognized their great responsibility to make sure the manifesto was exact. They also found it would cost $8,800 to send the container to Russia. That was $8,800 they didn't have!

With this added responsibility, they started to pack each box as tightly as possible by rolling every item of clothing and placing a Russian Bible tract that gave the plan of salvation in each piece of clothing. Esther and Barbara worked every day through the week; Ed and Bob worked along with them every evening till about 10:00 PM. On Saturdays all four of them worked as a team for about ten hours. They hoped they could get the container shipped in time so that it would be there by the Russian Orthodox Christmas, which is in January. They knew the Russian winter was very cold, so they wanted to send as much warm clothing as possible.

Esther decided to contact the Kokomo Rescue Mission to see if they had any extra winter coats. At the mission she met Robert Cox, the executive director and Bebe Jo Dorris, the director of development, two people who would become very close friends with her and Bob. At that time the mission had a lot of extra coats and they were glad to be able to share them for the shipment to Russia.

After about a month of packing boxes, a large TV station in Indianapolis heard about the shipment of humanitarian aid going to Russia and they came to the warehouse and took pictures and interviewed Esther. They aired the interview and pictures of the volunteers in Kokomo packing boxes to help Russian families. After that, so many more donations came in that the team knew they had enough to fill the forty foot-long overseas container.

About a week before the team finished packing the boxes, the McCauley's and the Browns met to talk about what all of them had been thinking about, "Where will we get the $8,800 to ship the container to Russia?" Throughout the entire process, not one person had given a cent for shipping. People had been generous with gifts of clothing, medicines and food, but no money. When the question was asked, Bob answered, "We don't need the money yet. It will be there when we need it." With that, the team seemed satisfied and continued working. However, Ed decided to contact the Governor's office and see if they had access to funds for shipping humanitarian aid. Of course, he didn't get to talk to the Governor, but one of his staff said they would look into it. Unfortunately, Ed didn't hear anything more from them.

One evening a few days later, they had finished packing everything and loaded the boxes on skids to the height and width of a container and measured them. There was exactly enough to fill a forty-foot container. They knew they were ready to send the shipment, but they still did not have any money. By then it was late in the evening, and the Browns and McCauley's went home for some much needed rest.

Shortly after the McCauley's arrived at home, their telephone rang, and Esther answered. It was Ed Brown, telling her he just got a call from a shipping company in Toledo, Ohio, and he asked Esther to contact them. When Esther returned the call, the person on the other end introduced herself as Linda Green. She and her husband, Stan, were the directors of an organization that sends humanitarian aid to other countries. She went on to say, "We heard you have a shipment of supplies to send to Russia. We have the money to send a shipment, but we don't have the supplies. We will send a shipment for you, but we ask that one third of the shipment go to a Pentecostal church in Moscow."

Esther was delighted to hear this because she knew this was God providing a way to ship the supplies. Esther explained to Linda that most of the supplies were going to an orphanage, which Yuriy had contacted for them; however a few boxes on the shipment were to go to Yuriy's family. Esther went on to say, "We would be very happy to send one third of the shipment to the Pentecostal church."

Linda reminded Esther that it would be their responsibility to get the shipment to the warehouse in Toledo. When Esther shared the news with Bob, he was happy, but not surprised, because he believed God was going to supply. Then Esther called the Browns back and gave them all the details. They too were very thankful and amazed at God's timing. He had supplied their need exactly when they needed it. The next day Esther contacted Syndicate Sales in Kokomo and asked if they would take a shipment for them to Toledo. They said they would take the shipment for $500. The Browns and McCauley's agreed that $500 was an affordable price and asked them to do it as soon as possible.

Three days later, a big, green Syndicate Sales semi-truck and trailer was parked in front of the warehouse where the supplies for Russia were sitting on skids ready to be loaded and shipped. Reporters from the local newspaper were also at the warehouse taking pictures and interviewing many people who had come to help. Robert Cox, from the Kokomo Rescue Mission, was directing and working alongside the helpers. There were a few hundred spectators standing around just watching. It was a very important day for everyone because this was the first shipment of humanitarian aid from the people of Indiana to the Russian people after the Iron Curtain came down.

It only took about an hour for the forklift driver to load the skids onto the semi-trailer. When the truck driver got into the cab, Esther went to hand him the $500.00 check, and he said, "No, I can't take that money; I am giving my time to drive this truck, and Syndicate Sales is offering their truck free of charge." What a testimony of God's provision! Esther started to weep as she walked away. The McCauley's and Browns greatly appreciated what Syndicate Sales did to help deliver the humanitarian aid to Russia and Esther wrote an official thank you letter to them. The McCauley's and the Browns will never forget that exactly when they needed it, God provided a way to ship the container to Russia at no cost to either family. He did exactly as He promised to do in Philippians 4:19.

Philippians 4:19 And my God will meet all your needs according to the riches of his glory in Christ Jesus. (NIV)

Esther walked away from the big truck with tears in her eyes, and she watched the Syndicate Sales driver start the large engine and slowly drive out of the parking lot and head for Toledo. She thanked God for all He had provided to fill the container and how He used her to help send the first shipment of aid to go out from Indiana to Russia. She felt so blessed. God again brought to her memory the verse in 1 Thessalonians 5:24.

1 Thessalonians 5:24 The one who calls you is faithful, and he will do it. (NIV)

God truly had done this.

Bob and Esther wanted to be at Stan and Linda Green's warehouse in Toledo by 7:00 the next morning when the Syndicate Sales truck arrived. They hurried home, got a little rest, and left at 1:00 and drove through the night to Toledo. They arrived at the warehouse at 7:00 AM as planned. When they arrived, the big green Syndicate Sales truck was sitting at the warehouse ready to be unloaded. Stan and Linda soon arrived and he and Bob started unloading the skids from the semi and putting them into a forty-foot overseas container. A couple hours later, the skids were all loaded into the container. A week later, the container was on a ship on its way to help people in Russia.

After they finished loading the container, Stan and Linda invited Bob and Esther to come home with them and get some sleep, since they had driven most of the night to get there that morning. The McCauley's accepted the offer, and after a few hours sleep, they got up and had a good visit with the Greens. As they were chatting, Linda told them that she and a group of medical personnel were going to Russia in January and that Esther was welcome to join them.

Bob and Esther had already talked about Esther going to Russia to make sure the shipment of supplies went to the right place. They knew the goods on this shipment were worth about $180,000 and wanted to have proof that the orphanage and the Pentecostal church received the shipment. This offer to go to Russia with Linda and her team would fit in perfectly with their plan for her to go and check on the container.

That evening Bob and Esther took the Greens out for dinner and then spent the night at their home. After church the next morning, the McCauley's drove home to Greentown, Indiana. During the trip home, they talked about all that had taken place during the last month and a half. They knew they had obeyed God by sending this shipment of humanitarian aid to Russia even though it was a lot of work. Esther spent hundreds of hours organizing people and packing items, and now they would be glad to have things go back to normal.

Little did they know that this was not the end, but the beginning, of a new ministry for both of them, but especially for Esther. She would be making twenty-six trips to Russia and packing thirteen more containers for the people of Moscow. She would be helping to start a large ministry in Moscow as well as in St. Petersburg, Russia. She would also be in the Middle East and India and have a large ministry in her hometown of Kokomo. God was by no means finished with the ministry of the little girl from the logging camp, He was only beginning a completely new adventure for her.

God's Faithfulness: A Journey in Trusting

1) Esther in Logging Camp

2) Esther during Bible School years

3) Esther and her family at her Bible School graduation.

4) Bob & Esther McCauley's wedding 1985

5) Loading container for Russia

6) Esther going into Russian sewer

7) Esther in Russian sewer

God's Faithfulness: A Journey in Trusting

8) Dinner for street children

9) Esther in boy's prison in Russia

10) Bob teaching in Russian prison for boys

11) Esther teaching in Russian prison for boys

12) Esther with Russian orphan girl

13) Esther and Vera with Russian orphans

14) Vera with street boy

15) Vera & Sasha & Esther

16) Esther feeding children in India

17) Bebe, Esther, Lena, & Bob

18) Sasha & Galina Zdor

19) Olga & Esther

20) Nickolai & Marina Kornilov

21) Bob & Esther & their children

22) Bob & Esther's children & spouses

23) Bob & Esther McCauley 2014

Chapter 14
OFF TO RUSSIA

When Robert Cox heard that Esther was going to Russia, he asked if it would be possible for him to go as well. Robert had been very interested in helping the Russian people, and he felt this would be a great opportunity for him to see how he could get involved. Both Esther and Linda were glad to have Robert come with the group.

The day before Esther left for Russia, she got a call from an NBC television station in Indianapolis. They had heard she was going to Russia and asked if she would take a video camera and film the distribution of the contents of the container, as well as any other facet of Russian life that she encountered. Esther felt this was of the Lord, so she told them she would do it, but she had no idea how to use a video camera. She had never even held one before. Very calmly they said, "On your way to the airport, stop in for the camera and we will give you a lesson on how to run it."

When Esther saw the video camera, she could hardly believe how big it was. She had her hands full with her carry-on and purse, and now she would have to look after and carry the big camera that said NBC in big letters on both sides. The NBC official gave Esther a few instructions and then turned the camera over to her.

Bob took Esther with the camera and her luggage on to the airport in Indianapolis, where they met Robert. Esther and Robert boarded a large airplane and flew to New York where they met Linda Green and her team. Everything went well until they arrived in Holland where they changed planes; the officials told Esther she could not carry the camera on the plane but would have to put it in the hold. Esther knew she could not allow that because they might damage it or lose it, and she would be responsible to NBC. The officials demanded that they put the camera in the hold, so Esther and the team members started praying.

Then Esther spoke up boldly and said, "I simply will not allow you to put the camera in the hold. It is a fragile piece of equipment, and I am responsible for it." After arguing quite vehemently, they very reluctantly allowed Esther to keep the camera. She was so thankful to the Lord. Shortly after this incident, the team boarded the plane and settled down into their seats. Esther put the big camera on the floor in front of her seat and looked down at it for a few seconds thanking God that she still had it with her for their final leg of the flight to Moscow.

Although it was only four o'clock in the afternoon when they arrived in Moscow, it was already dusk, and everything looked very dull and dreary. Here they were in the largest airport in Russia, and they were the only plane on the tarmac; what a contrast from Kennedy Airport in New York where just a day before, huge planes were taking off and landing every minute. Even though everything was very different and strange, Esther had to admit to herself that she was excited to be in Russia; however, she was also rather apprehensive because she still felt like she was the little girl who was raised in the deep forest of British Columbia, and here she was in Moscow, on the other side of the world.

The team had no problems getting through customs, and two Christian men from the Pentecostal church helped them put their luggage into two Russian vans. These men then made the one-hour drive from the airport to a high-rise apartment building located on the southern edge of Moscow. They ushered the team to two different apartments where they would be staying. The two nurses from the medical team and Esther stayed in the home of the Pentecostal pastor, named Sasha

Zdor, and his wife, Galina, who lived on the second floor of the large apartment building.

The men stayed in the home of a Baptist family on the fifth floor of the same building. Both families had five children, and their apartments were not large, but they made room for the group to stay with them. Both of these families would become close friends with Robert and Esther, and they would play a big part in each other's lives in the years to come.

Shortly after Esther met her hosts, Sasha and Galina Zdor, she asked them about the shipment, knowing that one-third of it was to go to their church. Sasha told Esther that the shipment had arrived. His church had already received their portion of it, and the rest was at the orphanage where it was intended to go. Everything had worked out perfectly when the shipment arrived in Moscow. Esther was very happy about that.

Robert and Esther went to the orphanage that received part of the shipment, and they were very pleased to see the boxes she and others had worked so hard packing in Kokomo, Indiana. As Esther looked at the boxes, she knew every piece of clothing had a Russian tract in it that gave the plan of salvation. Esther had the big NBC camera with her, so she videoed the orphans and boxes. The team of six also went to several orphanages taking food, clothing, and special treats for the children. Esther took many video pictures everywhere they went.

The team participated in several "home group" church services, as well as one at a Baptist church in an actual church building. Their hosts also took them to visit other Christians with whom they had prayer and sharing. The medical team was in Russia for only two weeks, but Robert and Esther stayed on for six weeks. They were there during the months of January and February. The weather was very cold, and food was rather scarce and hard to get. If a person did not get bread by noon, they would be unable to get any that day.

Esther saw firsthand that things in Russia were just as Yuriy had described them to the newspaper reporter in Kokomo. Not only was food scarce, everything else was as well. The price of food and other items were about the same as in America, but Russian wages were very low. A high monthly income would be equivalent to forty American dollars, but few actually made that much. Esther loved the people and felt sorry for them because of the very difficult economical situation in which they were living. She wished she could help all of them, but she knew it would be impossible; however, she would do as much as she could.

Chapter 15

INVITED TO THE KREMLIN

When Robert and Esther were at the orphanage, they met some Russian government officials who invited them to visit the Kremlin on a given date and a hospital the day after that. These officials were giving them a privilege that few Americans have ever had. Esther was surprised that she, the little girl who grew up in the forest of British Columbia was invited to visit the highest governing body in all of Russia.

Pastor Zdor and his family lived near the southern edge of Moscow, so it was a long way from their apartment to the Kremlin, which is located in the center of the city. Sasha and one of the members of his church named Olga, who could speak English, drove them there in Sasha's car. They arrived at the entrance of the Kremlin a few minutes before 10:00 AM, and the three government officials were waiting for them.

The officials opened a large iron gate and the group walked into a complex of buildings, different from any Esther had seen in America or Canada. They were huge, dark brown brick structures that had a very definite Russian look about them and had their own beauty. A large beautiful Russian Orthodox Church, with its polished brass steeples, was also located in the Kremlin complex. The sun was shining on the steeples, and they looked like pure gold.

After walking about two city blocks, they came to a very large building that seemed to be one of the main ones in the complex. The Russian officials led them through a large door into a beautiful foyer. From there, they were led into meeting rooms and offices, the officials explaining what they were used for. Esther could understand most of what they were saying in Russian, but Olga was also interpreting for them, especially for Robert. This all made a huge impression on Esther as they walked through the area where high officials governed all of Russia. She was overwhelmed at the depth of Russian history she was experiencing.

The Kremlin tour took about two hours, and then they returned to the beautiful foyer they first entered. It was all very interesting to Esther, but she knew it was now time for her to give their Russian host the gifts she brought from America for each of them. Esther knew from her years of growing up in a Ukrainian / Russian community in Canada that it was customary to bring a gift to someone when you visited them, so she brought eleven Russian Bibles to give to her hosts. Esther knew the officials were probably atheists because they had worked for the Communist Party, but she felt it would be acceptable to give them each a Bible. There were three officials providing the tour, but she had brought all of the Russian Bibles she had, thinking there might be others to whom she could give them.

At a break in the conversation, Esther pulled three Bibles out of her bag and handed one to each of the officials. They gladly accepted them and seemed to appreciate her gift. There were other men in the foyer watching Esther give the Bibles to her hosts, and they came over to look at her gifts. She could see they also were interested in them, so she gave each of them one and they gladly accepted them. She thanked the Lord that she had just enough Bibles for everyone. Then one of their hosts spoke to Esther in Russian and said, "Esther, you are the first person ever to give Bibles away inside of the Kremlin." Esther was very surprised at his statement, but more than that, she realized God was using her to spread His Word even inside of the Russian Kremlin.

Leaving the building, they visited Lenin's tomb and watched the changing of the guards at the tomb. Then they visited a very large museum filled with all kinds of historical artifacts dating back many years into the Russian history. Both Esther and Robert found the tour very interesting. When it was finished, Robert and Esther thanked the officials and told them they would see them again tomorrow at 10:00 AM at the location they had been given.

Early the next morning, another Russian man they had met, came to Sasha and Galina's apartment to lead them across Moscow using the bus and subway system. This trip took about an hour and a half, and they arrived at the given location right on time. Again, the three Russian officials were waiting, this time with a very dignified lady, who appeared to be in her mid-forties. As soon as Esther and Robert arrived, she walked over to them and said in perfect English, "My name is Olga and I work for the Kremlin. I will be your interpreter today when we visit the hospital." Olga had a sweet smile and pleasant attitude that made both Robert and Esther feel very comfortable being with her. Esther liked Olga from the first time they met. Little did Esther know that Olga would become a very close friend in the coming years.

The three officials and Olga led Esther and Robert to a place where a large Russian van was waiting to take them to the hospital. As they got into the van, Olga made sure she was sitting beside Robert and Esther so she could tell them things about the city as the driver was taking them to the hospital. Although Esther appreciated all of the information Olga was giving them, she kept thinking about why they wanted them to see the hospital. From a previous conversation with the officials, Esther thought she knew why but was not quite sure. The officials knew they had sent a lot of medicine on the shipment, and they also knew the value of the items they shipped was very high. Esther thought they wanted Robert and her to see how poorly the hospital was equipped hoping she would send another shipment with more medical supplies and hospital equipment.

When they arrived at the hospital and started on their tour, Esther could see immediately that the hospital was very poorly equipped. The patients slept on straw mattresses and had to bring their own bedding. They had very little medical equipment and everything they had appeared to be at least fifty years outdated. Esther was quite shocked by what she saw, knowing that in America and Canada, hospitals were so much better equipped. They finished touring the first floor and then the officials wanted to show them one of the upper floors.

Their guide took them to a very old-fashioned elevator to ride up to the higher floor. They all managed to get in and it started to go up, but suddenly the elevator stopped between floors -- it wouldn't go up, nor would it go down. Obviously, there were too many people on it, and it wouldn't budge.

Finally, the head nurse and one of the doctors who were on the elevator with them, suggested that they open the doors and push Esther (who was the smallest and weighed less than anyone else) up and out onto the higher floor. It wasn't a safe or intelligent move, but Esther decided to do it. Everyone pulled the doors until they opened, and then several people lifted Esther up onto the next floor.

Almost before she got onto the floor, the elevator started to move. Two nurses standing on the next floor grabbed her and pulled her out onto the floor. Esther immediately thought, "Wow, that was scary," but she really got scared when she thought about it later. Her legs could have been cut off if that elevator had gone up before they got her out. She was so thankful to the Lord for His mercy on her.

One thing that made Esther especially sad was being shown an operating room where the head nurse told her very proudly that they performed eighty thousand abortions there during the last year. This was their form of birth control.

The officials and a few of the hospital staff, including a doctor, showed Esther and Robert the entire hospital. In their conversation, as they went from one area to another, it became very clear that they wanted them to send medical supplies, equipment, and medications. Both Robert and Esther got the feeling that the officials really wanted to help the people, but they could not do it properly because they could not get the medications and equipment they needed in Russia. They were desperately hoping Robert and Esther could help them.

When the tour finished, the government officials, with the hospital staff present, asked them to please send more shipments of supplies and medications. *Both Robert and Esther felt the Lord wanted them to tell the officials they would send thirteen more shipments to Russia.* The officials and hospital staff all seemed to be elated after they made the promise. Then one of the Russian officials said something that amazed Esther. He said, "For years we have watched the Americans, and the one thing we have learned about them is when they say they will do something, they do it. So we know you will do it!" The officials were very happy that Esther and Robert promised to ship more supplies. After this they got back into the van to be driven back to where the Russian officials and Olga met them earlier in the day.

As soon as they got into the van, one of the officials started asking questions about the Bible. He said he wasn't really interested for himself, as he was an atheist, but he had heard a lot about it and just wondered what it said. This was a great opportunity to witness, so Esther and Robert began to tell him the salvation story, and just as they were about to tell him about Jesus' sacrifice for everyone's sins, they got to their destination and couldn't finish the story. But Olga, their interpreter, came up to Esther and said, "Oh, I want to hear the rest of the story, but I have to leave for another appointment. Here is my card, if you need an interpreter again, please call me!"

Chapter 16
OLGA'S CONVERSION

The next day, Esther's host, Pastor Sasha Zdor, planned to take her and Robert to a village called Maloyaroslavets which was about 150 miles southwest of Moscow. They were going there to visit two of the pastors who had been imprisoned for their faith. Pastor Stefan was arrested and sentenced to six years in prison for preaching, and after his release, he started preaching again and was arrested and given six more years in prison. After his second release, he continued preaching and was arrested and given another six years in prison. He spent a total of eighteen years in prison for preaching the Word of God!

A younger man named Vladimir, who belonged to Pastor Stefan's church, starting preaching when Pastor Stefan was sent to prison the third time. He was also arrested and spent the next six years in prison. When the pastors were in prison, many other prisoners became Christians, and even some of the guards accepted Jesus Christ as their Savior.

Both pastors had lovely wives who also suffered terribly when their husbands were in prison. Pastor Vladimir's wife, Olga, was severely tortured in an effort to make her tell who the other Christians were. As a result of the torture, she had terrible scars on her body. The two pastors wanted to talk to Esther and Robert to see if they could help them start a soup kitchen and send some food and clothes to them as well.

Sasha had arranged for an interpreter to accompany them, but early in the evening, she called and said that she was unable to go. Esther remembered that she had Olga's card, so she called her and asked if she was available to go with them. Olga agreed to go and she would meet them at 6 A.M. at a designated place that was on the route they would take.

The driver and the van that Sasha hired arrived at 5:00 A.M. The van was in bad condition, and Esther was concerned that it might not make the trip. The seats were boards, and the floor had big holes in it; Esther could see the road under her feet. There was no heat, and it was a cold February day. Esther was so thankful for her warm boots, thick jacket, mittens, and hat. They also had one blanket, which helped. The cold reminded Esther of some of her days in the logging camp when she was young, but they always had heat in their vehicles and lots of warm clothes.

The van made the trip, and they arrived in Maloyaroslavets just before lunch. The driver, Sasha and Robert went into the simple, wood frame house first and then Esther and Olga. As Olga was going through the door, she suddenly stepped back and said, "Oh Esther, I feel a Presence here that I have never felt before." Olga had a startled look on her face and was looking around, but was only seeing the inside of the room. She said, "What am I feeling?" Esther said, "Olga, it is the presence of the Holy Spirit in this home." Olga replied, "Oh, I have never felt anything like this, and I have not heard of it." Olga and Esther walked on into the house and met Pastor Stefan, Pastor Vladimir, and their wives.

Their time with the two pastors and their wives in that humble little home was indescribable, as they shared some of their experiences. What a joy it was for Esther to see their love for the Lord. Their little cozy, warm home reminded her of her home back in the forest of B.C. with no electricity or running water. The borscht, a Russian beet soup that they served with fresh bread, was just like Esther's mom used to make. She felt right at home in this wonderful atmosphere and thanked the Lord that He was allowing her to be in Russia and to be part of this ministry.

The afternoon was spent drinking tea and discussing how Esther and Robert could help them. It was decided that they would receive part of the next shipment of food, clothing and medicine that they sent to Moscow. Esther had nearly forgotten the hundreds of hours she had spent in the warehouse packing boxes for the first shipment that came to Russia and how they had prayed to find someone to ship the container at no cost. All she could see now was the great need these people had, and both she and Robert felt the Lord leading them to let the Christians in Maloyaroslavets have part of the next container.

Around 5:00 in the afternoon they left to return to Moscow. Olga sat in the front with the driver while Robert and Esther sat in the middle and Sasha in the back. Esther was very tired and the van was just as cold, if not colder than before, and all she wanted to do was sleep. However, the Lord started to speak to her about talking to Olga about the Lord. At first she told the Lord she was "just too tired," but the Lord said, "I brought you here to minister, not to sleep. Talk to Olga." Esther tapped Olga on the shoulder and said, "Olga, do you want to hear the rest of the story?"

Olga immediately turned around as far as she could in the seat in front of Esther, looked her in the eye and said, "Oh, yes, Esther, I want to hear the rest of the story!" Esther knew Olga probably knew very little about the Bible story of Jesus Christ, or even of Adam and Eve, since she had been raised under Communism.

Although Olga had no knowledge of the Bible, she was a very intelligent woman who not only spoke her own Russian language, but also was very fluent in both German and English. She spoke English with almost no accent. Olga was also very gracious and kind, and her demeanor made Esther respect and love her from the onset of their meeting. Esther also found out that Olga's husband, Slava, which means "Praise" in

Russian, had been in charge of the Soviet Union's security when they put up the first satellite, named Sputnik, in 1957.

Esther began telling Olga about Adam and Eve and how they sinned. She told how everyone had sinned according to Romans 3:23. Then she told her about Jesus Christ, God's only begotten Son, and how God sent Him to die for our sins according to John 3:16. She told Olga about Jesus Christ's death and resurrection and many details of what took place concerning this. Esther could see that Olga was very intent, listening to every one of her words.

When Esther asked Olga if she wanted to accept Jesus Christ as her Savior, tears started flowing down her cheeks as she very firmly said, "Yes I do." Esther led her in the sinner's prayer as she accepted Christ as her Savior. Olga continued to weep as she repeated the words after Esther and kept weeping with joy after she finished.

Esther had never seen anyone whose heart was so ready to accept the Lord. Truly, Olga became a different person; she was so happy and thrilled and had so many questions about spiritual things that both ladies spent the rest of the trip talking about the Lord Jesus Christ. From that day until now, Olga calls Esther her spiritual mother saying Esther birthed her into Jesus Christ.

Olga became a tremendous servant of the Lord. She quit her translation job at the Kremlin and began translating for Christian organizations. The first Christian group she worked for was called Co-Missions. Co-Missions was a group of different missions, churches, and Christian organizations who had been invited by President Yeltsin to teach Christian ethics in the schools. President Yeltsin recognized that, under Communism, the people were not taught any ethics, and he was concerned for his country.

Many from the United States took advantage of this invitation and went to Russia to teach. Some stayed only a few weeks while others stayed up to two years. Olga had the opportunity to go to many schools and translate for many of the foreigners who were in Russia with Co-Missions. They paid Olga for her services, so it gave her some money to live on. It also gave her the opportunity to learn God's Word.

Olga went on to translate for the Billy Graham Association, as well as for several other Christian organizations. She continues to work for Doctor Bill, a Christian doctor from Georgia. Olga is now the director of his Medical Clinic and Pharmacy in Moscow. She has been involved in helping bring the Word of God to hundreds of people in Russia.

After Olga's conversion, she told Esther that she would love to have an English Bible, and though Esther looked and looked for one in Moscow, she was unable to find one. Esther's Bible was quite old and was all marked up with favorite verses etc., and though she hated to give it up, she knew the Lord wanted her to give it to Olga. When Robert and Esther went to the airport to return home, Olga went with them. During the trip to the airport, Esther handed her Bible to Olga. She was thrilled and said it would be one of her most precious possessions.

Chapter 17

THE FIRST PUBLIC BAPTISM

A week or so after their trip to Maloyaroslavets, Sasha told Esther and Robert that the Pentecostal Church in that city was going to have their first public baptism in seventy years, and they were invited to come and be part of it. Of course, this was exciting to Esther, and she didn't even care if they had to ride in a cold, drafty van for hours. She expected the service would be in the small log Pentecostal Church she had seen on their first visit to the village. The political climate in the country had changed and churches were allowed to baptize publicly; however, many people were afraid their freedom would not last, and they wanted to be baptized as soon as possible, even in the freezing temperature of a day in February.

Very early on the day of the baptism, they boarded the van, and once again made the trip from Moscow to Maloyaroslavets. The trip was just as cold, but Esther did not mind it as much because she was excited to be going to this church's first public baptism in several decades. When they arrived, they went directly into the small log church. It was filled with people, and they were all excited about the upcoming baptism.

They started the service with praise songs, and some of the pastors gave brief messages. Then they asked Esther to speak and sing a song. She gave a short testimony and sang a Christian song that she learned in a Ukrainian/Russian Church when she was a child. After the service, the whole church walked to the river, which was about two miles away.

When they all arrived at the river Esther could see it was mostly frozen over. Several men walked out on the ice, broke it up, and made an opening large enough to baptize four people at the same time. Esther knew the water had to be very cold since it had a thick layer of ice over it. She could also see there was a swift current flowing under the ice. She shivered as she thought of people wading out into the water to be baptized.

Before the baptisms, several Christians started playing hymns on a variety of musical instruments as a woman recorded the names of all who were going to be baptized. After the names were recorded, the music stopped and four pastors waded into the freezing waters ready to baptize the forty or so people. They were wearing white garments standing barefoot in six-inch deep snow at the water's edge, waiting for their turn to be baptized.

Esther knew they had to be very cold, but rather than looking miserable, they were all smiling and looked very excited about what was to happen. When the four pastors got into the water up to their waist, they motioned for the people to come out to them. Very quickly, four people waded out to the four pastors. Each pastor quickly baptized them in the name of the Father, Son, and the Holy Spirit.

Esther wept as she saw a very old lady stumble on the icy bank and get into the icy cold water in her bare feet. She slipped and almost fell several times as someone helped her to one of the pastors. Another younger woman had a big smile on her face as she waded into the waist deep water to be baptized. When she came up out of the water, she was still smiling, but she had a hard time getting up the bank as she slipped and nearly fell. The four church leaders looked very cold, but they were devoted to getting the people baptized as quickly as possible.

As each individual got out of the water, there was an elder's wife waiting to wrap them in a big towel or blanket and help them walk about 100 feet to shelter under a bridge where they would change into street clothes. Big heavy quilts and blankets had been hung under the bridge to give them privacy to change -- the women on one end and the men on the other. Then the people who had been baptized were led to a warm bus, where they were taken to their homes. None of the people had cars, so they had walked to the baptismal site and now, because they were so cold, they were being driven home.

What a joy it was for Esther to watch young men and women, as well as middle-aged and very elderly, come to profess their faith in Jesus Christ in the cold icy river. Tears froze on her cheeks as she wept and thanked the Lord for His faithfulness in allowing her to be part of this sacred occasion. One of the Russian men had volunteered to use the NBC camera to film the whole event including the church service and baptism. He did an excellent job of filming it. Today, as Esther views the baptism video, she still thanks the Lord that she was able to be part of that ceremony.

Robert and Esther were invited to many other places in Russia to see the great need in that country, and each time they felt burdened to get relief to those dear Christians. When Esther heard them tell about their needs, she would think about all of the clothes people in America get rid of each year because they are no longer in style or because they just want new things.

She also thought about all the medical supplies that were almost outdated in her country, but could be used in Russia. Then she would think about all the food that goes uneaten because it is almost outdated. Her heart was touched and she knew they had to help these people. The Christians in America could do it with the things they had available to them. Robert also thought about this and they both knew they had obeyed God when they promised to send thirteen more shipments to the Russian people.

Chapter 18

ESTHER'S VIDEO SHOWN ON TV

On their flight back to America, Robert and Esther thought about all that had transpired during the six weeks they were in Russia. Without a doubt, they both were sure God wanted them to help the Russian people. During their conversation, Robert asked Esther if she would join the board of directors of the Kokomo Rescue Mission. Esther said she would talk with her husband, and they would pray about it, and together they would make a decision.

Flying home, Esther had time to think about her life, starting from the time when the two missionaries came to her one-room schoolhouse. She had been so excited about Jesus Christ after she accepted Him as her Savior. She thought about her little Sunday school class and how she loved teaching the children. As she looked back at that time in her life, she could not help but think about how young she was. She was a child herself at age nine and ten, teaching a Sunday school class. Then she thought about her years in Bible school. She loved those years of looking ahead, dreaming about being a missionary in a foreign country.

She also remembered the tragedy following her brief time in South Africa and how she was plunged into deep grief, debt, loneliness, providing for two children, and feeling she could never be in the Lord's service again due to her situation in life. But here she was, on a big airplane returning from ministering in Russia. She even had the opportunity to be the first person to give away Bibles inside the Kremlin. She also thought about how those officials seemed so happy to receive them.

Once again, she was reminded of God's faithfulness to her and that many years before this, He gave her the verse in 1Thessalonians 5:14.

1 Thessalonians 5:24 The one who calls you is faithful, and he will do it. (NIV)

It was now so clear to her. God called her to missions, and He did what was necessary to bring it about. As she sat on that airplane, hearing the whine of the large jet engines propelling them through the sky at 500 miles an hour, she thanked God for His love for her and knew she could trust Him to help her in the future.

After reminiscing about what had happened in her life and getting some sleep, Esther was excited when the big airplane landed in Indianapolis. She and Robert walked into the terminal to meet their families who were anxiously waiting for them. It was so good for Esther to see her Bob, and he was very happy for them to be reunited and gave her a hug and a kiss. Then they made the one-hour drive back to Kokomo.

It felt so good to Esther when she walked back into her home again. Everything looked just as it did when she had left. Bob even had the home perfectly clean for her, and she felt so thankful that God had given her a loving husband. She thought about how thankful she was that Bob was willing for her to travel all the way to Russia and how he had supported her in this trip. There was so much sharing and catching up to do. Phone lines in Russia were not very reliable, and there was no email at the time, so they didn't have much opportunity to share while she was gone.

After telling Bob about all that had taken place in Russia, she told him about Robert Cox inviting her to come on the board of directors of the Kokomo Rescue Mission. Robert felt that the mission could partner with her, and together they could get thirteen more shipments sent to Russia. After praying about it, Bob and Esther both felt she should become a member of the mission's board. When Esther told Robert she would agree to be on the board, he was delighted, and told her he would present her name to the board as a possible new member.

Two days after Esther arrived home, she went to the NBC television station and handed them their camera along with the footage she and Robert had taken while in Russia. She didn't know if they had taken anything the station could use; she wasn't even sure their videotaping was good enough for them to use. A few weeks later, NBC called and told Esther they would be broadcasting a five-minute segment of her Russian video every evening on the news for five nights, and on Sunday evening, they would be doing a fifteen-minute segment. Esther was excited and anxious to see what they put together, and she called Robert and several of their friends and told them to watch the news.

The weeknight news that NBC showed was very informative of life in Russia, but the Sunday evening news was thrilling as they showed the Christians being baptized in the cold icy river. They also told the stories of pastors who were persecuted for their faith. The whole segment featured the Russian Christians. What a joy it was for Esther to think that God allowed her to be part of sharing the Gospel in such a way!

Some of her friends in Seattle even called and told her they saw it on their television station. Bob felt so blessed that God had used his wife, the little girl from the logging camp, to be a part of bringing glory to the Lord through the video she made while she was in Russia.

Not long after Robert submitted Esther's name as a possible board member, the board had a meeting and voted to accept her. Esther then asked them if they would let her use their facilities to pack the containers to ship to Russia. The board gave Esther their consent and blessing to use the back of their warehouse for packing the shipments. They even said that any extra clothes the mission could not use, could be sent to Russia.

Chapter 19
THE FIRST SEMINARY IN MOSCOW

Esther and her helpers worked long hours for the next three months getting the second shipment of humanitarian aid ready to go to the Christians in Moscow. She was tired a lot of the time, but felt so refreshed in her spirit knowing God was blessing what they were doing. During that time, the Lord provided an over-abundance of clothes, food, and medicine for the mission and for Russia. There was never a slowdown in packing because of a lack of supplies. Once again Esther and Bob purchased her a ticket with their own money, and she flew to Moscow to be there when the container arrived. Everything went as planned with the shipment, and the Christians received the supplies with appreciation and thankfulness to God.

On Esther's first trip to Moscow she had stayed with Pastor Sasha Zdor and his wife Galina. This time, she stayed with Pastor Nickolai Kornilov, his wife Marina and their family. While she was there, Nicolai told her that the Baptist Union Church and the Mennonite missionaries in Russia wanted to start a seminary in Moscow, and they wanted him to teach Russian Church History in the seminary. Nickolai had been a history professor, but when he became a Christian, he refused to teach evolution as part of history. As a result, the Communist government would not let him teach even though he knew world history well.

Nickolai told Esther that the church leaders wanted him to attend the Mennonite Seminary in Elkhart, Indiana, because they had the best Russian Church History program of any seminary in America. Esther knew the seminary was only about a two-hour drive from her home in Indiana, so she told Nickolai they could easily visit each other if he and his family did go to Elkhart.

The day after Nickolai talked to Esther, the Baptist leaders came to his home to see her. They were very humble and spoke to her sincerely and respectfully. Although the men were all neatly dressed, their clothes were quite worn, which told Esther they were very poor. Soon after Nickolai introduced them to Esther, everyone sat down and entered into a light conversation, asking about her family and other issues not related to what Esther knew they had come to talk about. During that time, Marina served them tea and pastries.

After everyone finished their tea, Nickolai spoke to Esther and said, "These men have a request to make of you." One man, who appeared to be the oldest of the group, spoke up and said, "Would you and your husband be the United States sponsors for Nickolai Kornilov and his family to come to America in August to go to the Mennonite Seminary? We want him to get a degree that will qualify him to teach church history in the new seminary in Moscow." She could see that the one man who spoke to her was speaking for all the men. Esther told them she would definitely have to pray about it and let them know before she returned home.

The next day Nickolai and Marina took Esther to visit the Mennonite missionaries. They also wanted Nickolai to go to America and get enough education to be well prepared to teach in the Russian seminary. They too, asked Esther if she and her husband would be willing to sponsor the Kornilovs. They told Esther that they were working on getting free tuition for Nickolai. As they were talking to Esther, she could see that they hoped for an answer before she left for home. She was overwhelmed as she thought about how great a responsibility this would be if she and Bob consented.

Esther knew the total cost to support a family of seven for two years would be several thousand dollars, and there was no way they could do it on their own. How she wished Bob was with her, but he was thousands of miles away, so she had to make a decision. Esther knew right away that she needed direction from God so she quickly prayed, "Lord, should we do it or should I refuse their request?" Immediately Esther heard the still small voice of the Holy Spirit speak to her heart and say so clearly, "Tell them you will do it." Esther knew her dear Lord had given her an answer, so she said, "Yes, we will do it."

Both the Baptist and Mennonite leaders rejoiced and thanked God, and Esther that she and her husband were going to take responsibility for all of the funds and details to get the Kornilov family to America for Nickolai's schooling. As they were rejoicing, Esther knew she had just committed Bob and her to a major financial responsibility that would last for the next two years. It was the first time she had made a major decision without Bob's input. He would be affected by this decision as much as she, so she hoped he would agree with what she had just committed both of them to do. Esther did have confidence that she had heard the still small voice of the Holy Spirit, so she believed it was going to work out well.

Two days after this meeting, Esther was on a long flight back to Indiana. She had lots of time to think. Even though she was very tired, her mind was racing through what had just transpired in Moscow. Every detail of the shipment had gone very well, so she was very happy about that. She was, however, mulling over every detail of how they could find a home for the seven Kornilov's to live in. Then they would have to work out the details of the children going to school in America. The children did not speak English and how would that work out? Not only would they need a house, they would need a complete set of furniture. She was certainly thankful that Nickolai's schooling cost was taken care of.

Thinking of how this was all going to work out sent Esther's head spinning. She also had to think about the twelve more shipments she promised to send to Russia. This certainly was a time when she had to trust the Lord to make everything come together. Even though she didn't know how it could be done, she knew the Lord told her to sponsor the Kornilovs and He would take care of the details. Esther was just thankful the Lord was using her, and with that in mind, she reclined her seat, covered up with the blanket they had given her, put her head on the pillow, and went into a sound sleep as the plane was taking her back to Indiana and to the man she loved.

The first leg of her flight stopped in Holland, and she was there for about four hours. Then she had an eight-hour flight to Chicago. By the time she got there and went through customs, she was very tired when she saw Bob. They hugged and told each other how good it was to be together again, and he lovingly gave her a kiss. It was so refreshing to see him again after being gone a month.

After getting her baggage, they went to their car and started out on the four-hour drive back to their home near Kokomo, Indiana. Esther wanted to tell Bob about the commitment she made for them to be the United States sponsors for the Kornilov family, but she was just too tired. She had not been in a bed for about twenty-four hours. Around 2:00 AM the next morning they arrived at their home and Esther went immediately to bed. It felt so good to be back home and be able to lie down in her own bed.

Chapter 20

THE ROADBLOCK

Esther woke up around ten o'clock the next morning and felt very refreshed. After she ate a little breakfast, Bob wanted to know some details of her trip. When Esther told him about her commitment to be the United States sponsors for the Kornilov family, Bob immediately got very concerned. He said, "Esther, you didn't promise them we would be the sponsors did you? We would be responsible for thousands of dollars for them to be here for two years!" Esther could see that Bob was quite concerned, and she said, "Yes, I did." Then Bob said, "Esther, you mean they are coming a year from this August, right?" When Esther answered, "No Bob, this coming August," Bob really got upset and said, "How could we possibly get everything together to do that including money for their living expenses?"

Then he asked, "Did you pray about this decision?" Esther said, "Yes I prayed about it, and I know the Holy Spirit spoke to me in His still small voice and said I was to tell the church leaders we would do it." After that, Bob completely changed his attitude toward the commitment Esther made for both of them, and he said, "We will start right away and let God lead us as we prepare for their arrival." Never again did Bob question Esther's promise to the Russian Mennonite missionaries and the Russian Baptist Church leaders. After that, he actually was a driving force, along with Esther, to let God use them in this endeavor.

After thinking about it for a short time, Bob asked, "Where do we start?" They both went to prayer and asked God the same question. Once again, the Lord spoke to Esther in His still small voice and said, "Form a board of directors." Immediately, she asked God to lead her to the right people, and He gave her the names of people to be on the board. They were the pastor of a local Mennonite church, a pastor of a Baptist church, the director of the Kokomo Rescue Mission, a bank manager, and their wives, along with Bob and Esther. She invited all of them to her home for coffee and dessert and told them the story of the Kornilov's intent to come to America. Then she asked each of them if they would be willing to be on a board of directors to bring Nickolai Kornilov and his family to America. Every one of them was willing to be on the board.

Esther made the two-hour drive to the Mennonite Seminary in Elkhart, Indiana and talked to them about Nickolai attending the Seminary. They already knew about the possibility because they had been corresponding with him and the Russian Mennonite missionaries. They even offered to rent the Kornilov family a five-bedroom house located across the road from the seminary for $500 a month. The house would have to be furnished, but Esther and Bob knew that could be done. Nickolai would be able to walk to his classes, and it would be a perfect house for the Kornilov family.

Then the whole process hit a roadblock. When Nickolai went to the American Embassy in Moscow to get a visa for him and his family to come to America, they turned him down. They told him they would let him go to America by himself, but there was no way they would let his family go with him because he probably would not return to Russia after he completed his training. If his family remained in Moscow, they were confident he would return. Nickolai quickly wrote a letter to Esther and Bob and told them about being turned down by the Embassy.

He said it was not possible to convince the embassy he would return to Russia with his family after he finished his two years of training in America. Bob and Esther were shocked by the news, but they also felt God wanted Nickolai to come to America to attend Seminary. After praying about this, they both felt they should fly to Moscow and talk to the American Embassy themselves. Possibly, they could convince them to give a visa to the Kornilov family.

It was only four months until August; the time to prepare for the Kornilov family coming to America was quickly passing, so Bob and Esther got a ticket to fly to Moscow as soon as possible. They were able to get a visitor's visa within two weeks and shortly after that flew to Russia. After getting off the plane, they followed the line of people into the customs area. Bob let Esther take the lead because he knew she could speak some Russian, and she had been there before. They got in a line of about ten people waiting to talk to the customs official. They saw that he was a young Russian soldier who was speaking very harshly to each person as they stepped up to his window. He was so gruff that some of the people were visibly shaking as they handed their documents to him. Bob could see that everyone had a look of fear on their face as they reported to the young official.

Bob did not know what he was saying, but Esther did. Quickly the time came for her to walk up to the official. Only one person could report to him at a time; the others had to stand behind a line about ten feet away from the official's window. Bob stayed at the line while Esther walked to the window. He wondered what she would do when she got there, but he was completely shocked at what he saw. When Esther was about two feet from the young soldier, with an angry expression on her face, she started shouting at him at the top of her voice. Bob had never heard her shout that loud before.

Esther threw her passport and visa down so hard that it made a snapping noise as it hit the official's shelf. Bob stood there in disbelief as his wife looked at the official with an angry look on her face and then quickly pointed back at him with her index finger, making a quick motion for Bob to come and stand beside her. Bob walked forward and stood exactly where she had pointed. He looked at the young soldier and saw that he was shaking and had a fearful look on his face. The soldier did not say one word back to Esther, but stamped their documents and motioned for them to go on.

Bob had never seen his wife act like this before! As they were walking to get their luggage he was thinking, "Who is this Esther I am married to? I did not even know she could speak Russian like that." Bob wanted to ask her right then what had just happened, but he felt it was best to let it go for the time being, and get their luggage and get out of there.

As soon as Esther and Bob got their luggage and entered the waiting area, they saw Nickolai with a big smile on his face and a gleam in his eyes that said, "I am so glad to see you." Nickolai was a well-built man who stood about six feet two inches tall with bright red hair. He loved the Lord and had a heart for the unsaved. Esther and Bob loved and appreciated him from the first time they met.

After giving Esther and Bob a big hug, Nickolai took them to his car, and they started on the one-hour drive to his apartment. During their drive, Bob was intently looking at the sights in Moscow as Nickolai was giving them the details of being turned down by the American Embassy. Also during the drive, Bob asked Esther why she shouted at the customs officer. Esther replied, "He was intimidating every person who walked in front of him, and this upset me. I knew the best way to deal with him was to intimidate him before he had a chance to do it to me. I started shouting at him before I was even up to his window, so he wouldn't have a chance to shout at me first."

"I told him that I had special permission from the government to bring in humanitarian aid, and he would see that my visa was stamped "Humanitarian Aid". I also told him that all he had to do was stamp my documents, and I did not want any trouble from him. Then I said,

'Furthermore, my husband is with me, and he does not speak Russian. I want him here by me right now.' That is when I motioned sharply for you to come and stand beside me. I saw immediately that he was shocked, stunned, and speechless, but that was okay. He never said a word, but stamped my papers, and we walked out." After hearing this, Bob was amazed at what Esther did. He thought to himself, "I could not have done that, but I am glad Esther did."

An hour later, they arrived at the Kornilovs' apartment and met Marina. Being a loving person with a personality that glows, made it a joy to be in her kitchen and visit with her as she prepared dinner for them. Marina was a lovely hostess and, shortly after they arrived, she served them a very nice Russia dinner. Esther had met their family before, but Bob had not, so he was very happy to meet all of them.

At four o'clock the next morning, they got out of bed, dressed, had a quick breakfast, and Nickolai drove them across the city to the American Embassy. They arrived at 5:30 that morning and already there were about fifty people in a large room standing in line waiting for the office to open at 8:00. As the time passed, more and more people kept arriving, and soon some were pushing hard to get in front of others in the line.

By the time the office opened at 8:00 A.M., there were at least one hundred people in front of them and more were coming and trying their best to get in front of others in line. There was an American man standing at the door into the office, and he would let in one or two people at a time. By 9:00 there was no longer a line, but the large room was packed with people pushing to get to the man guarding the door into the office. It was obvious that all of these people were doing everything they could to get into the office in hopes of getting a visa to come to America.

By 10:00 that morning, there were at least 200 people ahead of Bob, Esther, and Nickolai, and they were not getting any closer to the office.

People were pushing so hard they could hardly move. Esther thought about how they had come all the way from America to talk to the official who had refused to give a visa to Nickolai, and now it looked like they might not even be able to see him. Since the embassy only took people on a first come, first served basis, they could not get a reservation to see this official. If they came back tomorrow, the crowd could be as bad and possibly even be worse.

Bob and Esther felt that all they could do was keep waiting and see what the Lord would do. The hours passed, and by 1:00 that afternoon, Esther was getting tired, and they were no closer to the office door than they were four hours earlier. By 3:00 PM they were still near the end of the line, and Esther and Bob knew the office would close in one hour. There was no way they could get in unless God did a miracle. Bob had been praying about it and felt the Lord told him in His still small voice that He was going to get them in.

Then it happened! There was a small platform near one end of the room with a door behind it, and suddenly the door opened, a man stepped out and yelled in English, "Are there any Americans here?" Immediately Esther and Bob held up their hands and yelled, "We are Americans." Esther quickly looked around, and no others were holding up their hands. They were the only Americans in the group. The man yelled in English and Russian, "Let those two people through." The Russians moved back enough that Esther and Bob were able to get up to the man standing at the door waiting for them. When they got there Bob quickly said, pointing at Nickolai, "That man is with us." The man on the platform told the people to let that man through as well.

When Nickolai made his way through the crowd and to the man at the door, he told him the name of the agent they needed to see. The man pointed to that agent and said, "You may see him just as soon as he has an opening." Bob looked over at the agent and saw that he was busy talking to a Russian young man at the time. The agent was sharply dressed in a suit and tie, and appeared to be about 45 years old. On his face was the stern look of a man who was in control.

About five minutes later, the Russian young man got up and walked away, and the three of them walked to his desk. When the agent saw Nickolai, he said, "I remember him, and I don't want to talk to him again." Pointing at Nickolai, he said, "You stand over there." Nickolai immediately walked to where the man was pointing, and Esther and Bob sat down across the desk from the agent.

The agent knew that they were there to ask him to let Nickolai and his family come to America. Before Bob or Esther said anything, he said, "If I let this man go to America with his family, he will not return to Russia, and we will be stuck with feeding and caring for them because they will go on welfare as soon as they get off of the plane." Bob spoke up and said, "He is a Christian and he will return with his family as he says he will." The agent spoke back harshly and said, "Christians are the worst of the lot, and they do not return." Disappointedly, Bob thought "That did not go over well at all."

Then the agent said, "If you can prove to me he will return to Russia after his schooling, I will let him and his family go to America." Bob said, "How can I do that?" He gruffly replied, "That's your problem, not mine." Then he said, "Also, I will not let him go unless he has $25,000 a year to live on, so he will not go on welfare when he gets there." With that, he put up his hand and pointed to the way out, so Bob and Esther knew the interview was over. They got up and walked over to Nickolai, and the three of them walked out. They were all rather discouraged and confused as they made the hour drive back to Kornilovs' apartment.

It was about 6:00 PM by the time they arrived and told Marina what had happened. They all felt that Nickolai, Marina and their family were to go to America, but they had come to an impassable object called the American Embassy. As Marina was preparing dinner for them, Bob went to their room and prayed, "Lord, what do we do? Where do we go from here?" Almost instantly, a plan formed in his mind.

He told Nickolai he wanted to have a meeting with the leaders of the Baptist Union Church and with the Mennonite missionaries. He also wanted to have meetings with the director of the Russian Ministries organization that Nickolai worked for, the president of the new seminary that was being established in Moscow, and the head pastor of Nickolai's church. He asked Nickolai to do this as quickly as possible, so he could talk to all of them before he and Esther returned to America.

Nickolai quickly set up the meetings for the following day. The first person Bob met with was the director of the Russian Ministries, and Bob asked him, "Why do you want Nickolai Kornilov to go to America?" He replied, "I don't want him to go because he is so valuable to our ministry here." Then he went on to say; "However, I feel the most important thing for him to do is to go, so he can get qualified to teach in our new seminary."

Bob asked if he believed Nickolai would return with his family after he finished his schooling. He immediately said he knew Nickolai would return. Bob asked if he would be willing to put that in writing on his ministry's letterhead, and give it to Nickolai. He immediately agreed to do that.

Following that meeting, Nickolai took Bob and Esther to meet with all the other people he had listed. Bob asked them the same questions and got the same answers, and each of them agreed to sign a statement on their letterhead and give it to Nickolai. After Bob finished with the meetings, he told Nickolai to keep the signed documents and to take them with him the next time he went to the American Embassy.

A few days later, Bob and Esther were on a plane heading back to Indianapolis. They still did not know what all God was going to do to get the Kornilov family to America, but believed He was going to do it. However, they knew that once they were home, they needed to ask each member of their newly formed board of directors the same questions Bob asked the church leaders in Russia.

Soon after they arrived back in Indiana, Esther invited each of the board members to come to their home for dinner and a meeting. During the meeting, Esther gave the board the details of their trip to Russia. Then Bob asked each of them if they would write and sign a statement on their letterhead telling why they wanted the Kornilovs to come to America and why they believed they would return after Nickolai's schooling. They all gladly agreed. Esther and Bob also gave their personal guarantee that they would take full responsibility for the Kornilovs to return to Russia after Nickolai's schooling was finished and for their finances while they were in America.

Esther and Bob told the board how the agent said the Kornilovs had to have $25,000 annually for living expenses while they were in America. What happened after that was amazing! God, and it was God alone, made all the finances come together, and within a few days, they had pledges for the entire $25,000 per year. The details of this support were written on an official form for the American Embassy in Moscow. Bob and Esther sent the signed statements from each board member and the details of the finances to Nickolai. He took the documents to the agent in the American Embassy in Moscow. The agent very carefully went through each document and then issued visas for Nickolai and his family to go to America.

Every person involved in the effort was elated that the Kornilov family was approved to come to America. The whole procedure had taken a lot of effort on Esther and Bob's part, but it was worth it to see God's will accomplished. They both knew that without Him opening the doors, it could not have happened.

Esther and some of her friends started the process of furnishing the five-bedroom house for the Kornilovs. This included dishes, kitchen utensils plus every other necessity they would need. Within a few days, the house was completely set up including pictures on the walls. They had toys for the children and clothes for every member of the family. Even the refrigerator and freezer were full of food. All the Kornilov family had to do was walk into their furnished home in Elkhart, Indiana.

The last week of August 1994, the Kornilov family flew into Chicago and went through customs with no difficulty. They met Robert Cox and the McCauleys who were there with two vans to take them to their home in Indiana. Two hours later, they drove into the driveway of the Kornilovs' new home. When they entered the house, they were very pleased and surprised to find that everything was ready for them. Esther had also taken care of the details for the children to start going to their school which began in a week.

The school was even going to have special classes for the children to help them learn English. Nickolai was very happy about only having to walk across the street to attend his classes, which started a week later. The Kornilovs and every person involved in the effort to get the family to America clearly saw that God had worked out every detail to get Nickolai qualified to teach in the new seminary in Moscow.

Chapter 21
OFF TO INDIA

After getting the Kornilovs settled in Elkhart, Esther and her helpers started on the third shipment of humanitarian aid to Russia and worked very hard, as they had on the two preceding shipments. In the midst of these preparations, Esther got a call from a man named Larry Rice who was the director of New Life Missions in St. Louis. This ministry not only met the needs of the poor in their city, but they also had a Christian television station and supported a Christian ministry in India. Larry asked Esther if she would go to India and do some consulting work for them.

They were supporting three orphanages and a leper colony with $3,000.00 a month. They wanted someone to spend some time with the Indian director, visit the orphanages and leper colony, and bring back a report to their board of directors. Larry and his wife had a teenager daughter named Stephanie who was taking a photography course, and she would go along with Esther to take pictures.

Esther never wanted to go anyplace or do anything without Bob's blessing, so she told him about the request and the two of them prayed about it. Bob immediately felt the Lord was saying in His still small voice that Esther was to go. Esther called Larry back and told him she would go, and they made plans and worked out the details for the trip. Esther did not want the packing for the third shipment to Russia to stop, so she asked the women who were helping her to continue working on the shipment while she was gone.

Because New Life Ministry was paying for Esther's fare, she planned the flight to go the cheapest way possible, which meant she had six layovers. It took two nights and three days to get there. Both Stephanie and Esther were completely exhausted by the time they got to their destination. The director of the India New Life Ministry, Paparo, picked them up at the airport in Visakhapatnam. From there they had a four-hour drive to Kakinada, where the ministries were located and where Paparo and his wife lived.

Paparo and his family of four young children insisted Esther and Stephanie stay with them in their small two-bedroom home. They were wonderful hosts to Esther and Stephanie not only feeding them delicious Indian food, but also sacrificing beds while they were there. In August and September India was extremely hot, and although they had fans, the electricity was off so much of the time that the girls literally slept on wet bed sheets most of the time.

Although Esther had seen poverty in Russia, she had never seen anything as bad as in India. Their whole lifestyle and religion led them into severe poverty and darkness. Satan had complete control of the country. Everywhere they saw food set before idols; food that should have been given to hungry children. They saw "sacred cows" destroying the rice fields and contaminating the water supplies. And worst than that, they saw "throw away" children. Many children who were born with some kind of physical defect were literally left on the street to die.

Esther had a very difficult time trying to understand why the people let these children die, but she finally figured it out. Because the people believe in reincarnation, they believe the child will die and come back as a better person. Sometimes a person would see a starving child and feed them, and then someone else might feed them, but nobody wanted the responsibility of the child. The child might live, but because of such poor nourishment, would not thrive.

Esther and Stephanie were taken to an area where seven or eight children, between the ages two to four years old, were left to fend for themselves. The children sat in a circle (not one of them spoke), and they gave them food and drink. Esther was heartbroken to see those dear children and to know she could not do anything to help them. She could see that Pastor Paparo had done a wonderful job in providing food, shelter, and medical help for many children in his three orphanages, but there were so many more than he had space for in his orphanages. Paparo had organized the people in his church to cook and serve food to hundreds of children each day. It was Esther's privilege to go with him and some of his congregation to feed the children on the streets.

Paparo's three orphanages were completely full. One orphanage was for boys, while the other two housed girls. Girls, two to eight years old, were separated from the older girls. Everything was very organized, immaculate, clean and orderly. Not only were the children given the best physical care, but they were also given love and spiritual training. There were several that Esther would have liked to put in her suitcase and take home.

Paparo also took Esther to a leper colony he cared for. Once a month, he and some of his congregation would go in and provide food for each individual for the whole month. They gave each one a bag of rice, a cup of salt, a few tins of meat and fish, and some vegetables. Esther was appalled at the physical deformities of most of the people; some had no feet or hands, others had no fingers, toes, or nose. It was a horrible sight and Esther wept as they left the colony.

She felt so sad for the children - Paparo wanted to take the children away from the mothers because, by staying with the mothers, the children would get leprosy as well, but many mothers could not bring themselves to give up their children. Esther was so thankful that Paparo and some of the elders gave a message of salvation before they left. Never had she imagined that the Lord was going to allow her to be in a leper colony praying for these dear people, but He did!

One day Esther went with Paparo and a team of doctors and nurses to a village several miles away to treat the sick. Paparo, Stephanie, and Esther went ahead of the team to try and find a place to set up the equipment; they offered to pay a homeowner to let them use his front porch, but he was afraid they would treat an "undesirable" in his home, and he would be contaminated. The result was they had to use the back of the van for their table and found a couple of old chairs for the sick to sit on.

While the doctor and nurse treated the people, Paparo and Esther were able to give them Gospel tracts and talk to them about the Lord. Stephanie told the children Bible stories and gave each of them a piece of candy from a big bag of sweets. Some people asked Esther and Paparo to pray for them; some for healing, and a couple asked Jesus to come into their lives.

The Lord also opened the door for Esther to go to several church services to share with the congregation and pray with the people. On several occasions, Esther was asked to pray for healing for different individuals, and she prayed trusting the Lord for His touch on them. Even so, it was a surprise to her when she received a letter from Paparo after she got home saying that several of the folks she prayed for were truly healed. Once again she praised the Lord for His faithfulness in allowing her to be used in India for His glory.

Shortly after Esther returned home, she got an urgent phone call from Paparo. He told her that the Bubonic Plague had hit their area and many people were dying. They were in dire need of Tetracycline and rubber gloves. One dose of Tetracycline could cure a sick person. As soon as Esther hung up the phone, she told Bob about Paparo's need. Bob said, "Let's pray for God to supply $1,000 worth of Tetracycline for Paparo," and they held hands and asked the Lord to supply the medication. They knew they could buy rubber gloves, but it would have to be the Lord who supplied the Tetracycline.

Later that day, Esther went to the rescue mission to pack items for the shipment to Russia. Other people were already there packing clothes - some people she knew and others she didn't. Esther's friend, Bonnie Sparling, was standing near her, and Esther told her about the phone call earlier in the day and the desperate need for Tetracycline.

She was about to ask Bonnie to pray with her about this request when one of the other ladies who was packing came up to her and said, "Excuse me, I couldn't help but hear you talking about your need for Tetracycline for India. I am a pharmacist and my husband is a medical doctor. We can get you Tetracycline." Within a few hours of Bob and Esther's prayer, the Lord supplied $1,000 worth of the much-needed medication.

The next day, Esther got a call from the rescue mission in Peoria, IL telling her they had a whole warehouse full of medical supplies that she could have, if she would just come and get them. Bob and Esther rented a box truck, drove to Peoria and picked up all the medical supplies. Among the medical supplies were hundreds of boxes of medical rubber gloves. God supplied everything they needed not only for Russia but for India as well.

Chapter 22

PRESIDENT OF RESCUE MISSION BOARD

When Esther became a board member of the Kokomo Rescue Mission in 1993, it was a thriving, but fairly small rescue mission. Their main building, a brick two-story built around 1910, contained offices, a chapel, a kitchen, and dining room on the first floor and upstairs bedrooms for 15 homeless men. For several years the board had talked about the need for a new facility, and had contracted to buy an adjacent property, which had previously been the location of a gas station. Preliminary plans had been drawn for a building to fit on that lot. However, a long delay was caused by the owner's reluctance to pay for the ground clean up necessary to complete the sale.

The board and staff started to pray in earnest for God to show them what to do. Within weeks, they were offered a piece of land across the street from the mission, containing two lots. The property was big enough for them to build a facility where the ministry could be expanded and improved. The board and staff were amazed at how God had answered their prayers, and they had a special time of thanking Him for what He did. And not long after, the filling station lot was cleaned up and the purchase completed. One lesson God had made clear was when He doesn't give us what we think is needed for His ministry, He always has something better in mind.

The board of directors and mission director Robert Cox hired a firm to design a new building and get an estimated cost to build it. The price came in at just under two million dollars. In 1994, the board authorized a capital campaign to raise the money. During the early stages of the project, the board needed to elect a new president, and Esther's name came up for that position. Once again, she would not give them an answer without talking with Bob, and both of them praying about this decision. Esther was already very busy spending hundreds of hours packing the shipments of humanitarian aid and traveling to Russia to make sure they were distributed correctly.

Also, Esther was very hesitant because she felt she was not capable of leading a board of directors especially as they were embarking on a building campaign. It was a huge responsibility. Esther spent a lot of time crying out to the Lord about this decision. She only wanted what God wanted her to do. She didn't want to be president for the title or for any recognition; she wanted to make sure she was doing this because God had called her to be ministering in this capacity.

After much prayer and sharing with some of the board of directors and the rescue mission staff, Esther and Bob decided she should take the position if the board of directors elected her. As a result, Esther's name was brought before the board and voted on as a president. The vote was unanimous for her to be the next president.

Once again, she was overwhelmed that the Lord was using her in this manner. She could hardly believe this had happened! She was not even an American citizen at that time. Esther later got her American citizenship, but she was a Canadian when this came about. In her heart, she was still the little girl from the logging camp, but God had put her in a place of leadership far above her abilities.

Esther knew that she did not have the training or experience to lead a board of directors, so she was going to have to trust the Lord for wisdom and help. He not only gave her the ability, but He also gave her a dear friend, Bebe Jo Dorris, to be a great help. Bebe served as director of development through Esther's four years of presidency at the Kokomo

Rescue Mission. They spent many hours together speaking at churches, civic functions, and to factory workers to raise money for the building.

During this time, they had special times of prayer and fasting for this need. God blessed, and hundreds of people either gave a large gift or made a promise to give a certain amount each month. After almost three years, they had enough cash on hand and pledges made to start the process of building a new building.

Before they started to dig the foundation, the mission had a groundbreaking ceremony and many people from the community came, along with reporters who took pictures. As president of the board, Esther was asked to be one of the speakers, and God gave her wisdom and helped her speak very professionally. Then Esther, the vice president, Robert Cox and one of the mission residents were each given a shovel, and they dug out a little dirt as the reporters flashed pictures.

In September 1998, they had the joy of dedicating the new Kokomo Rescue Mission building. Robert Cox, the vice-president, the mayor, honored guests, and Esther took part in the ribbon cutting. They were each given a pair of scissors and, when the right time came, they all cut through the thick red ribbon at the same time. The building was now finished, and almost instantly it became very instrumental in helping the staff minister to many more people who were living in crisis in Kokomo, Indiana and the five counties surrounding the city.

The Kokomo Rescue Mission's main building has a kitchen and dining room, open to the public, where they serve hundreds of meals a month to the needy. It contains a chapel, classrooms, and offices for the staff. This new facility houses men who need a place to stay and will commit themselves to long-term Christian discipleship programs. The mission has a separate facility for homeless women and children, a halfway house for women, and a thrift store. Esther spent several years on the board of directors helping make decisions for the rescue mission. She always felt it was her privilege to serve the Lord and her community in that way.

Chapter 23

THE LAST SHIPMENT & THEN TO THE MIDDLE EAST

Nickolai Kornilov finished his classes at the Mennonite Seminary in the spring of 1996. The family returned to Moscow, and Nickolai started teaching in the new Russian seminary. A few years later, he and his family returned to America so Nickolai could earn a doctorate degree qualifying him to teach Hebrew in the Russian seminary. Nickolai's ministry in Russia has been a tremendous success. He not only teaches in the seminary in Moscow but also holds teaching seminars all over Russia from far up north in Siberia to Russia's southern border near Mongolia.

His ministry through the years has touched thousands of people's lives, and many young pastors have benefited as they sat under Nickolai's teaching. Bob, Esther, and the board of directors who helped Nickolai and his family come to America are thankful they were able to play a small part in his ministry. They also love and appreciate Nickolai, Marina, and their family very much.

The fourteenth shipment arrived in Moscow shortly after Nickolai and his family returned back home following their stay at the Mennonite Seminary. Up until then, Christians did not have trouble getting the shipments into the country; although, the paperwork was getting more difficult and complicated. However, things changed, and by the time the fourteenth shipment arrived, it took a lot of time and trouble getting it through customs.

They finally received that shipment, but they believed it would probably be impossible to receive another one. As a result, Nickolai told Esther not to send any more shipments. The promise Esther and Robert made to send fourteen shipments was completed. God had worked a miracle and supplied all that was needed to fulfill their promise.

As a result of receiving the food, clothing, and medicine included in those fourteen shipments, Russian Christians were able to help many people during a very difficult time in their country and it gave them an opportunity to give out the Word of God. Nobody knows how many people came to know Christ through this ministry, but many received the Gospel who otherwise would not have had that opportunity. The total value of the shipments was about two million dollars. Esther knew God had blessed them in sending that much aid to the Christians in Russia. At one time, it was impossible to go to Russia, but by the time the shipments had finished, Esther had been there fifteen times.

About a month after the fourteenth shipment arrived in Moscow, Esther received a phone call from an organization asking if she would be willing to take a team of five young people to the Middle East on a six week backpacking trip in early June and July. All five of them wanted to visit the Middle East, and two were seriously thinking about studying there.

The young people were planning to travel from one end of a particular country to the other taking only a backpack of clothes and personal items. This organization wanted a mature adult who had experience traveling in foreign countries and able to lead and keep young people from danger and out of trouble as they traveled.

Bob and Esther discussed this opportunity and decided it was something Esther could surely do, so she told the organization she would take the team on the trip. She bought herself a backpack and filled it with necessary items. A short time later, Bob took her to the airport in Indianapolis and she flew to be with her team. The team spent five days of orientation and then flew to the capital city, where friends of the organization met them and took them to a very cheap hotel. They stayed there for several days while they took some language study to help them on their trek across the country.

The team traveled by bus from one city to another looking at the beautiful landscape as they went. They were able to experience living in a different culture, and they found the people they met in the stores and shops and in the streets to be very friendly. The team had very little money, so they stayed in very cheap hotels. Usually the bathrooms were at the end of the hallways, and they were public, one for the women and one for the men. This made the girls feel uneasy because they were afraid they might meet a man in the hallway if they had to go to the bathroom during the night.

Esther stayed in the room with the girls, so she told them to wake her if they had to go to the bathroom, and she would walk down with them. The girls appreciated this and they were not afraid if Esther was with them. One of the most difficult things for them was to sleep during the extremely hot nights. In spite of all this, they made it completely across the country, seeing all of the sights from the north to the south and then back to the capital. Without getting into details of the trip, the team saw many sights that most people never see, and one of the young people did go back to the country to live and work there full time.

The trek from one end of the country to the other took exactly six weeks, so by the time they returned to the capital, they were ready to get on the plane and fly back to America. Esther was tired when they got back to the organization's headquarters, but it seemed she was no more tired than the other younger members of the team. She knew she had made an impact on the lives of the young people during the trip. They had experienced some of the hardships of living in another country, and Esther believed some had matured a lot as they traveled and faced difficult living conditions and situations they had never faced before.

Two days after being back at the organization, Esther flew to Edmonton, Alberta and helped organize a 75th birthday party for her mother. A few days after she got there, Bob flew in to be with her. Esther and some of her family planned a very large party for Jenny. About one hundred people came, which included most of her extended family and many of her friends. It was a very happy day for Jenny and also a special one for Esther as she got to be at one of her family's events.

About a week later, Esther and Bob flew back to Indiana thinking that things would get back to normal since the last shipment had been sent to Russia. This meant that Esther would no longer be spending many hours packing items to send to Moscow and their lives could slow down.

God did not have this in His plans, however, and for years to come, they would be very busy in His service.

Chapter 24
THE LITTLE RUSSIAN GIRL WITH CANCER

Shortly after Esther returned home from Canada, she received a phone call from Linda Green. She told Esther that the eight-year-old daughter of their Russian friend, Pastor Sasha Zdor, was in the children's hospital in Columbus, Ohio and she had surgery for a type of cancer called Ewing's Sarcoma. Lena had three ribs, one half of a lung and part of her liver removed. She would have to have several months of chemotherapy. Stan and Linda's organization brought Lena to the United States for surgery. Now they needed a family for her to live with during her cancer treatment. Linda told Esther that Lena could speak no English and this would be a problem for her if she stayed with a family who could speak no Russian. Esther had been in the Zdor's home in Moscow and she knew Lena only spoke Russian. Esther knew that the cancer treatment would take many months and that it would be a major commitment if she told Linda that she and Bob would take Lena.

Esther was very tired from her years of packing aid for Russia, speaking in many churches and businesses to get funds to build the new rescue mission building, being president of the rescue mission board of directors, making all of her trips to Russia, the trip to India, and she had just returned from a difficult trip to the Middle East. She was tired and hoping things would slow down some, but here was another commitment for more involvement in the Lord's work that she needed to make.

Thinking about God's faithfulness through everything she had done in His service went over and over in Esther's mind. His faithfulness and the fact that He would do what was necessary to make it possible for a person to obey Him had become a solid fact in Esther's mind by this time in her life. She had been very tired before in the Lord's service and God had refreshed her body many times. There had been so many times when Esther had a special need in order to do something in serving the Lord and He had always supplied, whether it was for money or things she needed in God's work, such as furnishing about two million dollars worth of supplies for Russia and the funds to ship them. On top of that she vividly remembered how God had been so faithful and brought her out of the time in her life when she was left as a single mother facing what looked like an impossible future of feeding her children and paying her debts.

Yes, Esther was reminded how God had been faithful to her through the years. After some quick thought she said in her heart, "God will be faithful and give me strength and wisdom to take care of this little Russian girl through her cancer treatment." She told Bob and they called Linda and said that they would care for Lena.

Bob and Esther were told they needed everything in their house perfectly clean and free from any germs before Lena came to live with them. This even included the windows and the frames around them. Also, her eating utensils had to be sterilized with boiling water. They said Lena would have zero resistance in her system to fight off any germs, and if she caught anything, even a cold, it could kill her.

Esther contacted two of her friends and asked them if they would help her clean and sterilize her home the following day. They both agreed and spent a hard day doing the best they could to sterilize everything in the house.

The following day, Esther and Bob made the four-hour drive to the Columbus Children's Hospital to get Lena and her parents who had flown from Moscow to be with their daughter during her surgery. Esther and Bob had already requested a short meeting with the surgeon to get any first hand information that they would need while keeping Lena in their home. They knew the surgeon was a very busy man, but they hoped he would give them fifteen minutes.

When Bob and Esther arrived at the hospital, they were told that the surgeon would meet with them shortly. Lena's parents were already there, and the four of them were led to a very large conference room with a long beautiful table and chairs sitting in the center of the room. Soon after they arrived, the surgeon, two other medical staff, and a young woman entered the room. The young woman was a Russian/English interpreter for Lena's parents. The surgeon sat at the head of the table; the interpreter sat next to Sasha and Galina.

After everyone was seated, the surgeon began talking to Esther and Bob while the interpreter spoke in Russian for Lena's parents. Esther and Bob had hoped he would give them fifteen minutes, but he seemed in no hurry. He told them that Lena was a very sick little girl and he did not know if they could save her. He was very open with the parents. Sasha and Galina looked like they were about to cry. They also knew the doctors in Russia, who had examined Lena, said there was no hope for her, and had sent her home to die. At least the American doctors were trying to save their little girl.

The surgeon also told Sasha and Galina they had to officially give the McCauleys guardianship over Lena. They would have to sign a legal document and have it notarized. This was very hard for the Zdors to do; they didn't understand everything and thought perhaps they were going to lose custody of their daughter. It took some convincing from a Russian friend in New York that they were not losing their daughter, but that Esther and Bob had to have their permission to sign papers on her behalf.

The surgeon said Lena would have to remain in America for at least six months or more. He knew Sasha and Galina would be returning to Russia because they had four other children there, the youngest only two years old. As a result, someone in America had to be able to make legal decisions for Lena concerning her medical care.

Then the surgeon turned to talk to Esther and Bob about caring for Lena. They would have to make sure she was not around anyone who had chicken pox or any other illness, even a cold, because if she caught it she would most likely die. He said they would have to bring her back to Children's Hospital in Columbus, Ohio, every third week for her to have chemotherapy treatments. This proved to be a hardship that was difficult for Lena and Esther. Esther would take Lena to Columbus on a Saturday, and they would spend the night at the Ronald McDonald house.

Early Sunday morning, Lena would be admitted and the nurses would hydrate her for 24 hours. Monday morning she would start five sessions of chemo daily, and this would continue until Friday night. The nurses would begin hydrating her all day Saturday and she would be released on Sunday. On the four hour drive home poor little Lena would sleep in the back seat because she was completely exhausted. When Lena returned home with the McCauley's, Bob would have to give her shots daily for ten days. The doctor said that they would have to be trained to give her intravenous treatments if she came down with any illness.

The week before she was to go to Columbus for chemotherapy, Esther had to take her to a pediatric oncologist in Indianapolis for tests to see if her platelet level was high enough for another round of the treatments. The McCauleys were told that they would have to also monitor her temperature at all times, and if it went over one hundred and one, they had to take her to the children's hospital in Indianapolis immediately. After giving them this information, he let them ask questions. An hour later there were no more questions and then the surgeon said something that surprised Esther and Bob and stunned Sasha and Galina.

The surgeon said, "God is the only one who can heal. I am just a doctor, but He is the all-powerful One who made us. I want all of us to stand up and hold hands around this table while I pray for Lena and her parents, for the McCauley's, for myself, and the people who will treat Lena." The surgeon then started to pray, first praising God for who He was and thanking Him for His Son, Jesus Christ, who died for our sins.

He went on to pray for a full fifteen minutes asking God's blessing upon Lena and everyone who would be involved in her life. After the doctor's prayer, he shook hands with Bob, Esther, Sasha, and Galina and then went back into the hospital staff area. It was a very encouraging prayer for Sasha and Galina. Even though Sasha was a pastor, he had never heard a doctor pray like this before. This was also true for Esther and Bob and it was very encouraging to them as well. Sasha later told Esther and Bob this would never have happened in Russia.

Esther and Bob waited for the nurses to bring Lena out in a wheel chair, so they could take her and her parents to their home in Indiana. Lena had a big smile on her face as she was wheeled into the area where her parents and the McCauleys were waiting. Even though she was smiling, she looked so very frail with large black rings around her eyes. She looked so weak and sickly that Bob and Esther felt like crying when they saw her. They knew she would need the blessings of God to make it through this illness. Then they wheeled Lena to the car and all of them got in and made the four hour drive to the McCauley's home in Indiana.

Lena's parents stayed with Lena and the McCauleys for about two weeks and then returned to Moscow. It was a very difficult time for them to leave Lena and return back to their home and children in Moscow because they knew they might never see her again if she did not make it through her bout with cancer.

Bob and Esther's family, friends and neighbors all took part in helping the little Russian girl, who could not speak English, to feel at home.

The local newspaper did an article about Lena and that brought about many new friends into their lives.

Many times, Bob and Esther would look at Lena when she was asleep and wonder if she would make it through another day. She had no hair as a result of the chemo, was very thin, had huge black rings around her eyes, and looked like she was about to die. One time her temperature got above 101 and they had to rush her to the hospital in Indianapolis. They treated Lena and were able to bring her temperature down. After her treatment in the hospital Bob had to give her intravenous treatments three times a day for about two weeks. Each treatment took about an hour and this was a very difficult time for little Lena.

Even though Lena was very ill, she learned some English quickly and soon she could communicate with most of our family and friends fairly well. After about seven months a very special thing happened to Lena! Esther was approached by the "Give Kid's A Wish" Foundation, and said that they would like to send Lena, a friend and the McCauleys on an expense paid trip to Disneyworld in Florida. (Actually Lena's wish was for her whole family to come to the USA and go with her to Disneyworld, but that wasn't possible, so Lena was glad that she was able to go.) It was while Lena was at the Foundation in Florida, on the day of her 9th birthday, that the Dr.'s office called and told them that the tests they had taken of Lena before they left for Florida, came back with no cancer cells. They said that Lena was cancer free and could return to Russia in the next month.

Esther and Bob gave God thanks and glory as they wept in joy after hearing the report. In February of 1997, Esther took Lena back home to Moscow to be with her siblings and parents. Today, Lena is a strong, beautiful young lady who lives in Portland, Oregon and has no sign of cancer.

Chapter 25
MINISTRY TO STREET CHILDREN BEGINS

When Esther returned from her sixteenth trip to Russia, she felt that possibly it would be her last time there for a long time; however, her trips to Russia were far from being over. God was getting ready to use her in a ministry in Russia far above what she could have ever thought possible.

Shortly after Esther returned from taking Lena to Russia, she received a phone call from Phyllis Kilbourn, a woman she had known for years. Phyllis was the director of Rainbows of Hope, a WEC ministry to children living in crisis.

Phyllis asked Esther if she would go with a team of young people to Saint Petersburg, Russia, for six weeks and investigate the possibility of starting a ministry to children in prison. The team consisted of a married couple, a single girl and a single young man. Phyllis also said she would be going for a week to do a seminar about children in crisis for the local Christians. She thought perhaps Esther could help her with that, too. Esther did not give Phyllis an answer right away, but said she and Bob would pray about it --which they did. After praying, Bob felt Esther should go.

Phyllis wanted Esther and the team to go in late May of that year and she planned to go a week later. WEC would be responsible for getting visas and tickets from Philadelphia to St. Petersburg. Esther would arrange her own flight from Indianapolis to Philadelphia, where she would spend a few days with the team doing some orientation before going on to Russia.

In late May Esther flew to Philadelphia, went to the WEC headquarters and met the team and Phyllis. The orientation was a time of getting to know the rest of the team and spending time in prayer for the ministry that they would be doing. The day before the team was to leave, they received bad news. In St. Petersburg the Mafia had killed a female missionary who was working with street children. Now WEC was in a dilemma, "Should they allow this team to go? Was it safe?"

One of the team suggested that the team should pray together and then separately, and come back as a group to see how God was leading. WEC leadership agreed with this suggestion, and the team went off to pray separately. When the team returned from their personal time of praying, each one felt the Lord was telling them they should go. WEC then gave them permission to continue with their plans to go to Russia.

Phyllis had arranged for the pastor of the International Church in St. Petersburg to meet them when they arrived. Just as soon as they got through customs, they met the pastor, and he took them to a building the International Church was renting (they actually were only renting one floor). The church used the building for their offices and it had several small bedrooms, a bathroom for the men, and one for the women. The building also had a very small kitchen the team could use for their meals.

Upon arrival, the team had a short meeting with the pastor and their children's worker, Vera Zhuravleva. Vera was a pleasant, middle-aged lady who she spoke English fairly well. She was very well educated and had a degree in Russia that qualified her to teach teachers. The pastor and Vera gave the team some information concerning the area and then assigned rooms to them. After they left, the team was finally able to get some sleep.

The next day Esther found that it was going to take longer than expected to get permission to visit the prisons. However, the team was going to take part in the seminar Phyllis was teaching and they could all help in preparation for this. This delay would also give them an opportunity to learn the transit system and get to know the city.

A couple of days before Phyllis arrived in St. Petersburg, someone gave Esther a copy of a Russian newspaper that was printed in English. Esther was shocked when she saw the front page. There was a large picture of a child, between eight and ten years old, sniffing glue. This child was wearing rags for clothes and looked hungry. He had just glanced up at the camera when the picture was taken, and he had a look of hopelessness. The caption stated there were between 30,000 and 80,000 children living in the streets in that city, and it went on to give details about the homeless children.

Esther's heart was touched, and she nearly cried as she looked at the cold and hungry boy. She knew then that until the prison ministry was opened, they had to find and help the street children. That evening as the team met together for prayer, Esther showed them the newspaper article, and they all agreed they should go into the streets and find the street children and give them the Word of God and food. During their discussion, nobody even thought about the Mafia and the incident of the American woman being killed a few weeks before. They just saw the need and believed God wanted them to go.

Not long after this, Esther met a woman named Helena who had come there from Finland. She came to St. Petersburg as a missionary from her church, to minister to the street children. The Finnish Church knew there were thousands of homeless children living in the city and they wanted to help them. When Helena heard that the team was going to work with the street children, she asked if she could join them. She could speak some Russian, and that would be helpful to the team. Esther was very happy to have her come along. Helena and Esther became very close friends immediately after they met. It was obvious to both women that the Lord had brought them together.

Esther divided the team into two groups and found a Russian woman to interpret for each group. They discovered that the children would "hang out" at the Metro sites (subways) because they were crowded and they could steal or beg at these places, so it was decided that the teams would go to the Metro sites. Each group filled their backpacks with sandwiches, yogurt or bananas for the children. However, before they gave them any food, they were to give the Gospel story. Esther and Helena's goal was to continue the ministry to the street children, even after they were given permission to go into the prisons.

Shortly after the seminars were finished, Esther, Phyllis and the International Pastor discussed starting some type of ministry to help the street children on a more permanent basis. They agreed that they needed to have a Russian person as their director. They talked this over with the pastor from the International Church, and he suggested that Vera Zhuravleva would make an excellent director for this ministry.

Esther also felt Vera would be the perfect person for the job, and when she was approached about this position, she accepted willingly. They discussed a name for this new ministry and decided to call it "Project Hope" because it would give hope to children living in crisis. At that time, Vera was officially made the director of Project Hope, and it was on its way to becoming a well-known ministry to children living in crisis in St. Petersburg, Russia.

Chapter 26

MINISTERING IN THE SEWER

One afternoon, Esther and Helena went to a metro site to minister to the street children, but there was only one little girl who was begging at the main entrance. This was very unusual, but it was a very cold rainy day. Possibly the children had stayed where they did not have to get wet or cold. The little girl was dressed in a thin ragged dress and appeared to be about ten years old. Esther spoke to her in Russian and asked her where the other children were. She replied, "In the sewer." This shocked Esther and Helena as they had never heard of children being in a sewer before.

Esther asked the little girl if she could take them to the sewer. She replied, "I cannot because if I stop begging, I will not get enough money to take back to my father. Then he will not let me in our flat, and I will have to sleep in the street." Suddenly a little eight- year-old boy walked up and overheard the conversation. He said he would take them there. Esther and Helena thanked him and he started walking, with the two women following.

The little boy led them down a deserted road. The buildings were falling down and trash was in the streets everywhere. The boy was several yards ahead of the women when a black Mercedes car came quickly down the deserted path and pushed Esther and Helena against a brick wall. Immediately, the two women realized it was the Russian Mafia. The black Mercedes had the windows tinted so dark nobody could see who was inside. The car stopped before it crushed them and a man rolled down a window and shouted at the two women, "Where are you going?" Esther looked at him and saw he was wearing a black turtleneck sweater under a black leather jacket and she knew that was exactly how the Mafia men dressed.

Esther knew they were in trouble with the Mafia and she remembered how these same people killed a missionary woman about a month before this for doing exactly what she and Helena were doing. Esther explained that they were going to the sewer to give food to the children. The man gruffly commanded, "Stay away from them. We will feed them. They are our kids." Esther quickly looked in the man's car and said, "Do you have food for them right now?" The man had an angry expression on his face as he looked at them and said, "We will get food." Esther replied, "We have food in our backpacks; please let us take it to them."

The man sternly replied, "We will let you go this time but don't ever come back again." Esther replied, "We won't come this way again." She kept her word and did not come back that way again; however, they did go back to the sewer, but from a different route. The Mafia car slowly pulled away from Esther and Helena and they continued to follow the boy.

As they were walking, Esther and Helena had time to think and talk. Esther told Helena about the report of the woman the Russian Mafia killed because she was ministering to the street children. She also told Helena how WEC left it up to the team to pray about going on to Russia or staying home because of the danger from the Mafia. After praying, they all felt God was telling them they should go, so they left knowing they could be in dangerous situations.

As the two women continued to follow the boy, many thoughts were going through Esther's mind. She knew many missionaries in the world were living in very dangerous places, and yet they stayed there as God's Ambassadors. She made the decision right then that God had called her to St. Petersburg and she was staying. The Mafia was not going to chase her home.

She remembered how, when she was nine years old, she faced the dangers of being killed by a wild animal such as a moose or a bear. She decided back then that she was not going to live in fear, and she refused to let the danger stop her from walking to school or just playing in the forest. She had learned to spot a bear or moose before the animal saw her, and she did what was necessary to avoid it.

She would do the same thing in Russia. She would be on the watch for the black Mercedes cars that the Mafia drove and avoid them. She knew the Mafia was dangerous, but she was not going to live in fear. She was going to continue working with the street children with God's protection. Helena also made this decision.

Esther told the team what happened, and each one of them could make a decision as to what they wanted to do. Both Esther and Helena would go back to the sewer, but the next time, they would be very careful and come a different way, where they would not be seen.

Esther had been in Russia many times, and she learned why the Mafia wanted everyone to stay away from the street children. Pedophiles would come to Russia, and for a large price the Mafia would furnish them a little boy or girl from the street. Even the thought of this really angered Esther. She knew the Mafia wanted to stop anyone from ministering to the children because it might interfere with the way they were making money by using the children in this terrible way. Also, Esther knew they were using the children to supply body parts to people in other countries and they made a tremendous amount of money that way.

About ten minutes after the encounter with the Mafia, the little boy walked up to an open manhole that led down into a sewer and said,

"They are down there." Esther and Helena climbed down about ten feet on a rusty iron ladder into a dark room that was about eight foot square. Right away they were overwhelmed by the odor of sewer gas. At first, they could hardly see a thing because of the darkness, but when their eyes adjusted, they saw seven or eight children either lying or sitting on cardboard or boards which were laid across some pipes and stones to keep them above the sewage. It was a repulsive sight to the two women and it was hard to believe children were living in such deplorable conditions.

The children were surprised to see the two women in their sewer. Esther and Helena greeted them and took bread and boiled eggs out of their backpacks and gave them to the children. They quickly took the food and ate the bread first. Then they removed the shells from the eggs and threw them in the sewage on the floor and ate the eggs. Esther thought, "At home we would not allow a child to throw egg shells on the floor, but here the white shells looks very clean compared to the sewage."

Esther and Helena talked to the children for a short time and told them they came with the food because God loved them, and He sent them to bring food to the children. The women knew the children heard their words, but they felt it was hard for them to understand that God loved them when they were living in terrible conditions without enough to eat.

After being in the sewer for about fifteen minutes, Esther was starting to feel sick due to the sewer gas and decided to climb out and get some fresh air. She could hardly fathom how the children could live and sleep in a place that smelled so badly. She knew they were used to it; however, it had to be hard on their bodies. After the women climbed out, Esther cried because she felt so badly for the children.

One of the children also climbed out and saw Esther crying. All of the child's hair had been cut off, she was very dirty and was wearing rags for clothing and Esther thought she was a boy. Then the child spoke loudly and said, "Why are you crying?" Esther realized that the child was a girl and said, "Because I love you." The girl appeared very angry, and she hit Esther very hard with her fist and said, "Nobody ever loved me." Then she crawled back into the sewer. Even though she saw evidence of Esther and Helena's love, it was hard for her to accept because she had been rejected all her life. As Esther and Helena walked away from the sewer, they both felt they had to do something to help these children.

When the weather was bad, the children usually went into the sewer. On warmer days, they stood near abandoned buildings close to the metro stations, and Esther and Helena met them there. The women got to know each child and tried to minister to them each time by giving them food and the Word of God. It was obvious that many children lived in sewers all around the city. Esther and Helena knew the challenge to help them was far greater than what they were able to do, so they made it a matter of prayer asking God to give them wisdom.

As Esther thought about the situation with the street children, she felt that God Himself was leading her to become very involved in helping these hurting children. He saw their conditions and He loved them very much and wanted to help them. God confirmed this thought to her. The next morning when Esther was about ready to leave her room and go to the metro site, she had a strong feeling she should take a thin hooded sweatshirt she had in her suitcase. She could not understand this intense feeling because it was very warm outside, so why would she need a hooded sweatshirt that day. She tried to dismiss the idea, but the thought persisted, "Take the sweatshirt."

Finally, she picked up the shirt and put it in her backpack. Then, as she opened the door to leave, a tube of antibiotic ointment and a roll of first aid gauze fell off of the shelf in her room. Esther thought, "How could that have happened? I have opened and closed that door many times and it had not fallen off before, so why did it fall off this time?" This seemed to be more than strange to Esther, "Was God nudging her to take the ointment and gauze with her, in addition to the sweatshirt?"

With that in mind, she picked up the ointment and gauze and put them in her backpack.

As Esther was going to the metro site, she thought about a street boy named Kalill, who appeared to be about ten years old. He stayed in the sewer that Esther had visited and was always at the metro site and the first to try and get food. The last few days he had not been there, and none of the children knew where he was. As soon as Esther got to the metro site, she saw Kalill sitting on the curb, holding the top of his head, and moaning and rocking his body back and forth as if in tremendous pain. Esther walked up to him and said, "Kalill, what is wrong?"

He immediately showed her a large gash on the top of his head. He said the police had arrested him and hit him on top of his head with a club as he was trying to run away, and then they took him to jail and shaved his head. As Esther looked at Kalill's wound, she saw that his head had been shaved, and he had a deep cut that looked to be about four inches long. The worst thing was that it was filled with maggots.

Esther's heart went out to Kalill, and she sat down on the curb beside him and slowly dug the maggots out using "Wet Ones" that she always carried with her. She cleaned the wound the best she could and then applied the antibiotic ointment and first aid gauze to the wound. Then, to protect Kalill's head even more, she gave him the hooded sweatshirt and had him put it on and pull the hood over his shaved head. Esther made sure she saw Kalill every day after that until his wound was completely healed.

Esther could not have performed this act of kindness without the sweatshirt, antibiotic ointment and gauze the Lord led her to take with her that day. Esther knew, beyond any doubt, that God did this because of His love for Kalill and all of the street children. Kalill appreciated what Esther did so much that he had a tremendous love for her, and he later became a Christian. Life changed for Kalill, God blessed him and he ended up living with a family who gave him a good home.

Chapter 27

A CENTER FOR PROJECT HOPE

When Esther returned home to Kokomo, Indiana, she was still very burdened about the situation of the street children in St. Petersburg, Russia. One day, she was talking to her friend, Linda Hewitt, and sharing her concerns about the street children. Linda asked Esther what she would like to do to help them. Esther replied, "I would like to start a center that would run like a rescue mission for the children." Linda responded by saying, "Ed and I will give you $10,000 if you can raise that much."

Esther was astounded by the offer and thanked Linda, but she had no idea how she could ever raise $10,000. She also shared her concerns with her pastor, and he said he would give her five minutes on a Sunday morning to speak about her trip to Russia. The following Sunday, Esther gave a very powerful five minute speech telling of the great need of the street children. After she spoke, the pastor told the congregation they were not going to take an offering for Esther's ministry today, but he wanted everyone to go home, pray about how much they could give, and bring their offering to church next Sunday.

The following week, Esther drove to Pennsylvania to speak, and she was still there when the pastor took the offering for the Russian street children. The offering came to eleven thousand dollars. Bob was shocked when the pastor told him how much it was. Then the church mission department added four thousand, which brought the total to fifteen thousand. When Bob called and told Esther she could hardly believe it, but she knew God was faithful, and He had supplied the money. Both Bob and Esther saw God's hand in it and thanked Him for the funds.

When Esther met Linda after she came back from Pennsylvania, Linda asked her if she had the ten thousand dollars yet. Esther replied, "Yes we do. We actually have fifteen thousand." Linda's response was, "Then Ed and I will match it and give you fifteen thousand." Esther was so excited about Linda's offer that she could hardly believe it was happening. This meant she would have thirty thousand dollars to send to Russia to start a center for the street children. The children could come to the center and receive food, medicine, clothing and even an education. What a blessing this would be for them! Over and over, Esther and Bob thanked God for this provision.

While Esther was home in America, Helena stayed on in St. Petersburg working with the street children. Every day, she would buy food using her own money and take it to the children. She also wanted a place where the children could come for proper meals and have their needs met, as well as hearing the good news of Jesus Christ and what He did for them. When Esther received the thirty thousand dollars, she was anxious to get it to Helena, Vera, and the International Church Pastor as soon as possible, so she asked WEC if they could wire the money to Russia, since they had experience in this area. Within a few days, the money was in St. Petersburg!

Helena, the pastor of the International Church, and Vera were elated to get the funds. Right away, they started to look for a place they could rent and use as a center for the street children. The thirty thousand dollars enabled them to rent two adjoining apartments with a door between them for six months and purchase all of the equipment they needed to start a center where they could feed, clothe, teach, and meet all of the children's physical and spiritual needs.

Shortly after they opened the center, Vera registered it with the government as a ministry to street children. It was the first ministry of its kind to be registered in St. Petersburg. This all took place during the second week of December 1997. Within days, the center was abuzz with homeless children coming to the center for food, clothing, medical care, and Christian teaching.

Even though Project Hope was officially registered and opened to the street children during the second week of December 1997, Vera said Project Hope really started when Esther McCauley went into the sewer. Many Russian Christians were very surprised when word got around that an American woman came all the way to their country and went into their sewers to minister to their children. They, themselves, had never done that for their own children.

For years during the Cold War, Americans were portrayed as "cold" people who would never lower themselves enough to do this for a Russian child. Helena, from Finland, also went into the sewer, but this did not astound them nearly as much as when an American did. When word got around that an American Christian woman went into the sewer, other Russian Christians were encouraged to reach out to the children living in crisis in their city.

As a result, many Russian Christian young people came to Project Hope to minister to the street children. Then people came from other countries and soon there were many very dedicated Christian young people ministering with Project Hope, and the ministry started to grow. In addition, several other Christian groups in the city saw what Project Hope was doing for these children and they started ministering to them also.

There was a forty thousand dollar grant available in Finland to go to a registered and operating Christian ministry to street children in St. Petersburg. The money had to be given before the last day of December 1997, and many in Finland were concerned about the grant money being lost because there was no registered and operating ministry of this type in St Petersburg. As soon as the ministry was registered, Helena contacted her pastor, and he was so thankful they could send the funds to her for Project Hope. The Finnish Church rejoiced with Helena that she was working with a registered ministry to children living in crisis.

As a result, the new ministry received a total of $70,000, which helped them to keep Project Hope running for several months. Esther and Helena's prayers for a center were answered. A few weeks after Project Hope was registered, Esther went to St, Petersburg to help with some of the details in setting up the ministry. She was there for about a month. In the summer of 1998, Bob retired from his job, and he and Esther went to St. Petersburg where they rented a small two-bedroom apartment. The day after they arrived, they joined the work of the Project Hope team in ministering to the street children.

The ministry to the street children went very well in the two apartments with a steady flow of street children coming every day for the help Project Hope was giving them. For the first time in their life they were receiving proper food and physical and emotional help, plus they were receiving God's Word. They were also seeing that someone loved them, and most of them had never experienced this before. Some of Project Hope's staff, including Helena, went daily into the streets with food and the Word of God ministering to street children. The staff would then invite the children to come to the center, and many of them came.

After about three or four months, several neighbors complained to the building owner, saying they did not want this type of children coming into their area. The children never did anything to antagonize the neighbors, but still the complaints got worse as time went on. When the six-month lease was finished, the owner refused to renew it, and Project Hope had to relocate. The problem was that they could find no one who was willing to rent a facility to them to use as a center to minister to street children.

God's Faithfulness: A Journey in Trusting

During the first six months, some of the Project Hope staff met some young people from Youth With A Mission (YWAM) who were also ministering to the street children. As a result, the leaders of YWAM in St. Petersburg, Ricardo and Rachel Cyrino, met the leaders of Project Hope. Before this neither group knew the other was working with the street children, but immediately a friendship developed between the two groups.

Ricardo and Rachel Cyrino and their YWAM team had a center in the basement of a building near the city center of St. Petersburg. At one time, the basement looked like a dungeon, but Ricardo and Rachel rented and rebuilt it to be a fairly nice center where they could minister to the street children. After Project Hope lost their center at the end of June 1998, Ricardo and Rachel invited them to join YWAM in their center and become one larger ministry to street children.

Vera and Sasha, along with Helena, Bob, and Esther all agreed with this merger. They all felt it was of God, and He had directed them to do it. After some discussion, they decided to call the new merger Project Hope because it was already registered with the government. Also, they decided to have Vera continue being the director of the new and larger ministry. Esther and Bob became very close friends with Ricardo and Rachel. Both couples were delighted to be working together along with Vera, Sasha, and Helena.

In October of 1998, the owners of the building where the YWAM center was located said they wanted the space that Ricardo and Rachel had worked so hard to rebuild. The basement now had a small kitchen, classrooms, a bathroom for the boys and one for the girls, and a dining area. Suddenly, the ministry was faced with relocating once again.

The staff of Project Hope prayed and asked God to lead them to the right place. Finally, they found what they all felt was God's perfect location for the center. The building was in shambles. All of the plumbing and nearly all of the electric wiring had been torn out. It was a mess, but they all knew it could be rebuilt to meet their needs.

In December of 1998, Project Hope rented the larger facility of 5,000 square feet and remodeled it with a large kitchen, a dining room, several classrooms, a very large meeting room, a doctor's office, a wood working shop, and large bathrooms with showers. There were also offices for the staff and a huge playground outside which enabled the children to play ball and other sports. Most of the children had never had an open area to play games or sports before, so this was a special blessing.

The ministry had fulltime teachers, a Christian counselor, a doctor who came once a week, a social worker, cooks, and many volunteers who helped in any capacity they could. Also, a local dentist worked on the children's teeth at a reduced price. Daily, some of the staff went into the streets to find and invite the street children to come to the center. Many children came every day, and many accepted Christ as their Savior.

It was very difficult for some Russians to believe people would want to help the street children. Some wondered if the staff of Project Hope had some hidden reason for helping them and thought they had to be making money from them. Some of the police in the very early days of Project Hope also could not understand it either, but as time went on, they saw that these people loved the children and were helping them.

One day, the police were called to help three children, ages eight and younger, who had been thrown out an apartment window. The children's mother was a prostitute, and a very drunk man came to her apartment for her services. In his drunken state, he threw her children out of a window in her second story apartment. The children were all hurt quite badly, but the police had no place to take them other than Project Hope. The police drove the children to the center and asked the staff to care for them, which they did.

God's Faithfulness: A Journey in Trusting

Another time, a two-year-old little girl named Susha had boiling soup spilled on the right side of her face and shoulder by her drunken mother. The alcoholic mother refused to get medical help for her. As the wound healed it drew the right side of her face down tight against her shoulder, and it stayed in that position. It became impossible for the little girl to lift her head away from her shoulder. Not long after this, she started living in the streets because her alcoholic mother would not take care of her. When she was about four years old, she came to the center for food.

When Vera saw Susha, she felt very sorry for the little girl and took her to a doctor and asked if anything could be done to get her head off of her shoulder. The doctor said it could be done, but it would take a series of seven or eight operations and would cost a lot of money.

Vera knew that Project Hope did not have enough funds to pay for this surgery, so she and the staff made it a matter of prayer. When Bob and Esther returned to Indiana for a few weeks, they shared Susha's story in a newsletter. Not long after their newsletter went out, a young couple, Dale and Marjorie Martin, called and said that they were very touched by her story and wanted to help. They paid for every surgery Susha had until her head and neck were normal. Then the Russian surgeon said he needed to rebuild Susha's ear, and Dale and Marjorie also paid for that. After the surgeries were completed, Susha looked like every other child with her head positioned normally.

Susha's whole life was changed because someone cared enough to try and make a difference. First, God brought about Project Hope, and then Vera went to the doctor, Esther wrote the newsletter, and the Martins gave the money. All of this made it possible for Susha to have the operations. It was a team effort that started back when Project Hope was established.

A teenage street girl came to Project Hope to get food and Vera saw that she looked terrible because her front teeth were all very decayed. As soon as Vera saw the girl, she wanted to get help for her. A Russian dentist appreciated what Project Hope was doing to help the street children and he volunteered to fill the girl's teeth at a reduced price. Vera took the young girl to him and he did a wonderful job on her teeth. She had a pretty smile when he finished. This dentist told Vera he would do the same for any other street child who needed dental work.

When most of the street children came to Project Hope, they smelled bad because they had been sleeping in the sewers. Also, their hair was loaded with lice. Vera or someone else on the staff would shave their head to rid them of the lice and then have them take a shower and give them clean clothes. It was always amazing to Esther and Bob how different the street children looked when they were cleaned up. They looked beautiful.

Some children were living in the streets and sleeping in the sewers because their parents were alcoholics. Usually they had only one parent, and in most cases, it was a mother who was also a prostitute. Life at home for these children became unbearable, so they left and lived in the streets where they began stealing, begging or working for the Mafia to get enough food to eat. Vera believed she could help some of the parents as well, so she got some training from the Alcohol Anonymous (AA) organization in Russia. When she finished her training, she was licensed to form an AA group at the Project Hope Center.

Project Hope also had a full-time licensed social worker on their staff. She would try to locate the parents, grandparents, or guardians of the child. Many children were orphans, but some had a living parent or grandparent. However, nearly all of them were alcoholics, and could hardly care for themselves, let alone care for the child. Alcoholism was a major problem in Russia. Subsidized by the communist government, the price of vodka was so cheap a person could buy a big bottle of vodka cheaper than they could buy a Coke.

When the social worker located a parent or grandparent, she would invite them to the center for a Wednesday afternoon meeting. They were promised some food if they came, so most of them came. When they were all in the room, the smell of alcohol was almost unbearable. Vera did not let that bother her, but started the meeting with prayer, and then conducted the class according to the AA directions. Vera also conducted a Bible study including the salvation message during her class. Some of the parents or grandparents accepted Jesus Christ as their Savior and were born-again. The program was lengthy, but some of the people responded in a positive way and the street children were able to return to their homes.

As the years passed, Esther and Bob saw hundreds of street children come to the center to get food, clothing, medical treatment, teeth filled, Christian counseling, and most important of all, Christian love and Bible teaching. Most of the street children had never been to school, and if they tried to go to a government school, they were given a test to see if they could pass it at their age level. If they failed, the passport every child was required to have was stamped "Retarded," and that was on their passport the rest of their life.

As a result, it was nearly impossible for them to get a job. One of the goals of the Project Hope staff was to personally mentor each street child until they were able to pass the government test. The child only had one opportunity to pass it, so the staff worked with them for a long period of time until they could pass a sample test.

After the child was able to pass the sample test, the staff would take them to the government school and they would take the real test. Every one of them passed it and was accepted into the government school. Each time a child passed the test, the staff had a huge celebration for them.

Many of these street children went on to be the top students in their class. As an example, a boy named Igor, and his sister Svieta, lived in the streets when Esther first went to St. Petersburg. Then they came to Project Hope. After being mentored by the Project Hope teachers, they took the government test and passed. Then they both started in the government school and did very well. Svieta ended up at the top of her class in grade school, high school, and in college.

Today she is a very dignified, married woman with children of her own. No one would ever know by looking at her that she lived in a sewer at one time. Igor is the top supervisor of a large construction company. He started his building trade by working in the wood shop at the Project Hope center.

While Project Hope's ministry to street children was getting started, the request for permission to go into the prisons was accepted, and a ministry in two prisons for boys and one for girls was officially started. A Russian woman named Lyuba Vankova was hired as the director of the prison ministry. Every week she and her team of four people, which included Bob and Esther, would go into the three prisons and teach the Word of God as well as school subjects.

Lyuba had been a mathematics teacher, so she taught mathematics in the prisons while others taught subjects such as Russian History, the Russian Language, and English. Bob helped Lyuba teach mathematics and he also taught electric wiring and the Bible. Esther taught English using a Russian-English Bible. The inmates loved Esther's class because they knew they could get a better job after they were released if they could speak English.

Every time they went into the prisons, the team would take in some food. Sometimes it was bread, bananas, or yogurt and other times, it could be apples, boiled eggs or biscuits. The inmates received no fruit and hardly any bread so they brought some to supplement their diet. Once a month they would have a birthday party and give special treats to those who had a birthday that month. In addition, they would take in toothbrushes and toothpaste because the prison didn't have any to give the children.

The inmates only had the clothes they were wearing when they were arrested. Also, they were given no blankets to cover up with during the cold winter nights and some of the inmates did not even have shoes. As a result, Lyuba and her team purchased blankets and shoes for those who had none. The girl prisoners received no special items they needed, so the team purchased and gave those to the girls. All of this help was greatly appreciated by both the inmates and the prison officials because they had no money to buy such things.

One day, a women guard asked Esther and Bob to look at one of the boy's fingers. It was severely infected, and the doctor was going to amputate it the next day. When they looked at his finger, they could see it was badly infected. It had a hole in it right down to the bone. Esther and Bob said they had some very good antibiotics in their apartment that they could let them have to treat the boy. The guard said that she would like it if they could have the antibiotics, so Bob made the hour and a half trip back to their apartment, got the antibiotics, and took them back to the prison.

The guard gave the first dose of antibiotics to the boy right away. By the next day, the infection had dried a bit. The boy's finger continued to heal, and two weeks later, it was completely well. Esther and Bob always brought some antibiotics with them in case they personally needed them. They were not available in Russia at that time. This simple act of Bob and Esther helping to save the boy's finger caused many in the prison to appreciate them very much.

One time when Esther and Bob walked into the cell block, some of the boys started yelling, "Boob come see, Boob come see." (All of the Russians use a long "O" sound when they pronounce Bob.) The boys were very upset and they seemed to frantically want Bob's help. He went to see what they wanted and they pointed to a toilet stool that was broken off. Then they started saying, "Boob please, Boob please get!" Immediately, Bob knew what they wanted. Without that toilet stool, the boys had a big problem.

The prison officials knew the boys desperately needed the stool, but they had no money to buy one. Their prison budget was equivalent to ten cents a day in American money for each boy. This included their food, which left no money for any repairs. Bob knew where he could buy one, so he quickly talked to the prison officials to see if they would let him in if he and Esther went and bought one. Bob said it would take at least three hours to get there and back, and it would be far past visiting hours before they could get back with the toilet stool. The officials told Esther and Bob they would have a guard waiting for the stool at the prison entrance when they brought it back. The guard would take it to the boys, and they would mount it.

Bob and Esther immediately went to a hardware store and bought the stool for twenty- five dollars. They returned to the prison and gave it to the waiting guard. The next day, the boys were excited to see Boob and Esther. This time however, it was different. They wanted to show Boob the stool they had mounted. They were very excited to have it and thanked Boob and Esther over and over. This act of kindness gained the boys' trust and willingness to hear the Word of God that Bob and Esther so desperately wanted to share. The prison officials also appreciated their efforts very much

One day the warden of one of the boys' prison wanted to talk to Lyuba, Esther and Bob. When they went to his office, he told them how much he appreciated what they were doing. He said the number of inmates was decreasing, and they attributed it to the fact that they were having fewer repeat offenders. They were also having much less trouble in the cellblocks. The warden believed it was because of the Biblical teaching the boys were receiving. He also appreciated the team teaching school subjects to the boys and also for the food they were bringing. The warden then, very sincerely, thanked them for what they were doing in his prison.

Then the warden of the other boys' prison said a very similar thing. One afternoon, the warden of the girls' prison came to Esther and Bob as they were teaching and told them how much he appreciated what they were doing. He then said, "I hear you are going back to America in two weeks." Bob answered and said," Yes we are. We are going back to see our children for a short time, and then we plan to be back." The warden seemed to be pleased with Bob's answer and said, "I want you to know that these girls look to you two as being their parents."

This statement surprised both Esther and Bob, but it was also refreshing to know how much the girl inmates loved them. Later, Lyuba and Bob received word that they were to report to the top government official who was in charge of all the prisons and he also told them how much he appreciated what they were doing. All of this was very encouraging to Esther, Bob, and Lyuba.

A twenty-five-year old young man named Sergei started ministering in the prisons and Esther and Bob became very good friends with him. Sergei had been a prisoner in one of the prisons for boys, and he heard the Word of God during that time and received Christ as his Savior. When he was released he started his own business and later got married to a wonderful Christian woman. Sergei started coming back to that prison on a regular basis to teach the Word of God.

He and his wife also joined a very large Russian church and became active there. It was encouraging to Esther and Bob to see how God was using a man who had once been a prisoner himself and now he was teaching the Word of God to inmates. He could relate to them in a way few others could because he had accepted Christ while he was in prison.

Ministering in the prisons could be very difficult. The trip from Bob and Esther's apartment to the prisons took about an hour and a half each way on public transportation. They had to arrive there around 9:00 in the morning to check in. After that, they usually had to wait outside for about two hours before they could go in to see the inmates. The wait outside, at times, was almost unbearable due to the extreme

Russian cold. Many times it was so cold that Esther and Bob's feet and hands would feel numb as they stood there waiting for two hours.

There were some good times also. Bob and Esther got to know many of the inmates and had a tremendous opportunity to share Christ with them. Also, they became good friends with some of the guards and even had good fellowship with some of the wardens. Bob became a close friend with one of the top guards and he even invited Bob and Esther to his home for a meal. Many of the prisoners loved Bob and Esther very much and appreciated what they were doing to help them.

Chapter 28
"MAKE IT RUSSIAN, MAKE IT RUSSIAN"

In 2008, God started speaking to Esther and Bob in His still small voice saying over and over, "Make it Russian, make it Russian." Esther had been a leader in Project Hope from its beginning, and even though Vera was the official director, she still looked to Esther for leadership advice and direction. Now, Bob and Esther knew God wanted the ministry to be completely run by the Russians.

Also, around 2008, the economy of Russia started to improve. In addition, the Russian government started to help the street children and put them in orphanages or some facility where they did not have to fend for themselves. As a result, there were very few street children by 2009.

In 2009, Vera was asked to counsel some children in a Christian orphanage called Children's Ark. The director, a woman named Lidia, became a close friend of Vera. Children's Ark was built and mainly funded by Christians from Germany, and the executive director was a Russian Christian man named Jack Kerbs. He and his wife were wonderful Christians who had a burden to help orphans and other children living in crisis conditions.

Children's Ark invited Vera to come to their ministry and teach their staff how to care for street children. This resulted in Jack inviting Vera and her staff to partner with Children's Ark and come to work with them in their building. After this invitation, Esther and Vera came together with Jack, his wife and some of their board of directors for a meeting.

One of the first questions they asked Esther and Vera was, "Do you have the goal of bringing a child to a born-again life-changing experience through Jesus Christ?" Esther was pleased when she heard this question. Both ministries had the exactly the same goals and they officially merged. Project Hope's name was dropped because they were now part of Children's Ark. Vera and her staff, along with their children, moved into the Children's Ark building which was totally run by Russians.

God brought this all about in 2010, which was twelve years after Project Hope was registered and started. Today the ministry to the street children and the children in prison are both fully under the leadership of the Russian Christians. At this writing, it is very difficult to get a visa to minister in Russia, so Esther and Bob are thankful that the Russian people are now completely running the ministry.

Through the years Vera and her husband, Sasha, did a tremendous job of running Project Hope. Vera was highly respected and appreciated by the Russian government for her leadership of the ministry to children living in crisis. Esther and Bob respected her for her extreme wisdom in making difficult decisions. Today she and Sasha are holding seminars all over Russia, teaching Christians how to start and operate a ministry to children in crisis.

After Project Hope started, other churches and ministries in Russia saw what they were doing to help the street children and they started their own ministries to do this. Today, the ministry of Project Hope is listed and written about along with pictures in one of the Russian history books. Their history states that Project Hope was the first registered ministry to street children in Russia.

The prison officials also appreciated Lyuba and her ministry very much. Sergei continued to minister in the boy's prison through the years. Then the large church he belonged to wanted to get more involved in ministering in the prisons. In 2010, Sergei invited Esther and Bob to go to a midweek service with him. His church was a long way from where they lived so Sergei said he would pick them up in his car.

Esther and Bob accepted his offer, and on a Thursday evening, Sergei took them to a large theater where his church was meeting. When they walked into the theater, they could hardly believe how many people were there. It was a normal midweek service and there were about eight hundred people present. Most of them were younger people. The meeting started with about an hour of very intense praise and worship. Then there was a time of prayer and a message that lasted about two hours.

It was a very refreshing time for Esther and Bob. They could clearly see that this church preached the Word of God and had the personnel to take over the prison ministry. Bob and Esther knew the Lord was saying, "Make it Russian," and He was leading them to turn their ministry over to this church. They knew Sergei was already very involved in the prison ministry. Also, Bob had already talked to about six other people in his church who wanted to be involved with Sergei in his ministry. This was clearly God's answer: Project Hope would back out, and this church would take over.

This would also answer another problem. Lyuba had been spending three to four days a week in the prisons for twelve years, and she was getting very tired. The prison ministry was very tiring, and she felt she could not continue it much longer. With this large church taking over the prison ministry, Lyuba could retire. The prison ministry would continue and be totally run by Russians. Lyuba has since passed away, but during her years of leading the ministry in the prisons, many heard the Word of God, and some accepted Jesus Christ as their Savior.

The operating cost for Project Hope's ministry through the years was $5,000 to $8,000 a month. Esther and Bob did a lot of praying and trusting the Lord to send in that much money each month for twelve years and God always provided. They sent out monthly letters giving details and pictures of the ministry. God blessed, and enough money came in every month to cover the operating cost.

The total amount that God sent in during the twelve years was about one million dollars. Esther and Bob were amazed at how He sent in the money to keep the ministry going year after year. They never kept one cent of the money that came in for the ministry. God provided for them through Bob's retirement from his job and their savings.

Chapter 29

ESTHER'S WISDOM AND BRAVERY

Esther's journey in life serving the Lord started when she was nine years old, and she saw God's faithfulness over and over. When she was in her very difficult situation of working hard to support her family and pay the bills, she still trusted God to help her even though there seemed to be no way she could get out of her financial situation. God did deliver her and her journey in life of trusting Him continued.

Somewhere in Esther's journey of trusting in God's faithfulness, the Lord imparted to her wisdom and bravery beyond what many believers have. Through the years of our marriage I saw this over and over and was amazed. I will give a few examples.

The United States started bombing Serbia while Esther and Bob lived in St. Petersburg, Russia. Every day after that, the Russian TV showed scenes of American planes dropping bombs or shooting missiles at Serbian targets. Of course, they showed almost continuous scenes of Serbian civilians, including many children, who were severely wounded or killed by the Americans.

During the years when Esther was traveling to Russia to check on the shipments that were sent to Moscow, America was loved by most of the Russians. Even the government officials always treated Esther with the highest respect. After America started bombing Serbia, all of that changed to a dislike by some and hatred by many. The Russians loved the Serbians. They called them part of their family because they were both Slavic people. To them, it was like America was killing their family.

A few days after the bombing of Serbia began, an American man was caught on the streets in St. Petersburg and beaten so badly that he nearly died. Shortly after that, Esther and Bob got a phone call from the American Embassy telling them of the incident and giving some instructions to help keep them safe. For the next few days, if they heard any loud shooting or blasting outside of their apartment, they were not to look out the window because it could be a diversion to get them to look out, so they could be shot. They asked them not to go out in public for the next few days, and when they finally could go out, they were not to speak English.

The Russian Christians were also concerned about Esther and Bob's safety. They told them that Russians could easily spot American clothes, American eyeglasses, and shoes. Bob saw this one time when he and Esther were traveling on a Metro (subway). They were sitting on one side of the Metro car, and Bob happened to see a Russian woman on the other side pointing at his shoes and saying something to the man sitting beside her. She knew Bob was not a Russian because of his shoes.

Not long after the warning from the American Embassy, Bob and Esther came back to their apartment after a long day of ministering in a prison and at the center. When they walked up to the apartment entrance door, they were shocked to see words that had been freshly painted in English on the door. The words said, "Kill the Americans." Esther and Bob stopped in front of the door and stared at the sign for a few seconds. They knew the sign was for them because it was in English and also because they were the only Americans living in the apartment building!

After climbing the nine flights of stairs to their apartment, Esther and Bob had a long talk about how they would face this new problem.

They both knew God had called them to Russia, and He would look after them; not once did they consider going back home. They would, however, try to be as careful as possible.

Esther and Bob decided that every time they went in the public, Esther would do all of the talking. Sometimes she would even speak to Bob in Russian, and since he didn't understand anything she said, he would just nod his head as if he understood. Since Ukrainian was her first language, she spoke Russian with a Ukrainian accent, so the Russians always thought she was from the Ukraine.

Also, the Russians had a high respect for Canada, and Esther was born in Canada, so if she was asked where she was from she could tell them Canada. Bob and Esther knew it was possible that one of them could see danger before the other. They decided if this happened, the one who saw the danger would instruct the other one as quietly as possible, and the other would react with no questions.

One time this happened when Esther saw danger and Bob reacted to what she said with no questions. Vera and Sasha had a car, and one evening they took Bob and Esther back from the center to their apartment area. Esther got out of the car first, and then Bob got out. Then, he turned around and said to Vera and Sasha, "Thank you for the ride, and we will see you tomorrow."

Vera and Sasha immediately drove away and Esther spoke quickly to Bob, "Follow me," and she took off running as fast as she could through six lanes of very heavy traffic. The cars were all traveling very fast and she was dodging and running between them so fast that Bob could hardly keep up. Bob did not know what was happening, but he reacted exactly as they had made an agreement to do. He did not know it, but three Russian men were also running and trying to catch him. He did not see them behind him because he was dodging and running between cars trying to keep up with Esther.

When Esther got to the other side of the six-lane road, she jumped on a bus that was about to pull away from a bus stop. Then Esther grabbed the door and held it open long enough for Bob to jump on as the bus was leaving. Bob was wondering what was going on, but he did not say anything while they were on the bus. He just let Esther lead him. About two miles later at a bus stop, Esther got off and Bob followed her.

She started walking down the street, and when they came to an area where there were no people, Esther told Bob what had happened. She said, "There were three men right behind you when you turned around and spoke to Vera and Sasha in English. They heard you, and one of them said you were an American, and they should attack you. They were coming at you when I told you to follow me. I knew they were going to beat you badly if we did not get away. They might even have killed you!"

Bob realized if he had delayed even a second the men would have caught him and the results could have been disastrous. He was so thankful for Esther's quick action and wisdom in what to do to help him. He also realized he had made a major mistake by speaking in English in public. It could have cost him his life if it had not been for Esther's quick action. Esther and Bob decided to ride around on buses and metros for about two hours before they returned to their apartment in case the men were there waiting for them. Also, they would come in from a different direction and not go by the area where Bob and Esther got out of the car.

Not long after this incident, Esther got Bob out of another bad situation. One evening they returned back to their apartment building after a busy day at the Project Hope Center. Esther stopped at the foot of the stairs to check their apartment mail box while Bob continued walking up the nine flights of stairs, so he was a couple of flights ahead of her.

Bob was about half way up to their apartment when he saw a man standing on one of the landings. As Bob walked past the man, he grabbed Bob around the neck from behind. Bob could not tell for sure, but he thought the man had a knife pointed at his back. Just then, Esther turned onto the flight of stairs below him. She looked up and saw the man holding Bob, and she started shouting at him in Russian. Bob had no idea what she was saying, but the man did, and he replied back to Esther. She shouted back at him again, and the man replied in a calmer voice, let go of Bob, and walked down the stairs.

Esther and Bob continued walking up to their apartment. When they got inside and locked their door, Bob said, "Esther, what did you say to the man?" Esther replied, "When I saw him holding you, I thought he had a knife against your back. Then I shouted at him and said, 'What are you doing?' The man said you were from France, and you had money. I shouted back at him saying, 'I am Ukrainian, and he is my husband.'

Then he said, 'Oh, you Ukrainians are just as poor as Russians, so he doesn't have any money.' That is when he let you go and walked down the stairs." Esther considers herself Ukrainian because her family came to Canada from the Ukraine. No doubt, the man heard Esther's Ukrainian accent when she spoke Russian, so he believed she was from Ukraine.

Once again, Bob was so thankful for his Esther who got him out of another very serious situation. Shortly after this, when Bob and Esther got down to the bottom of the stairwell, they saw a handbag, coins, a knife, and blood all over the floor which caused both to realize how serious the situation with the man could have been. Then a few weeks later, they were told of a man who was robbed and killed in his apartment stairway. Bob thanked God for giving Esther boldness to speak up in this manner.

Just as little nine-year-old Esther was very mature for her age, now Esther seemed to have a God given maturity, wisdom, and boldness that astounded Bob. She was a small woman, only four foot ten inches tall, but sometimes she seemed like a giant when dealing with people. After years of observing this, Bob felt she had a God given ability to know how to do the right thing. It also seemed to him that the motivating factor in her personality was a drive and a love to serve her Lord in everything she did.

Her Christian love caused her to climb down into a sewer to minister to hurting children, dig maggots out of a street child's head, and stand for hours in subzero weather to bring the Word of God to a boy or girl in prison. It also caused her to work long hours packing clothes for needy people and do all she could to bring the Gospel to the lost. Her God-given wisdom and abilities made it possible for her to lead the Kokomo Rescue Mission board of directors through a large building program. Bob saw meekness in Esther and also that she felt insecure in doing many things, such as leading the board of directors. He saw her very sincerely pray, "Lord, I cannot do this on my own. I don't have the ability." Then Bob saw God give her the ability and great things happened.

At times she could be very firm and demanding, such as when she yelled at the customs officer and at the man who held Bob around the neck, possibly with a knife at his back. Other times, she could quickly think of an answer to a problem, such as she did to get Bob out of trouble when he was about to get beat up by the men who heard him speak English. And there were times when she could get people out of a bad mood and cause them to start laughing.

One day Esther and Bob had to get some documents signed by the Russian government. When they walked into the government office, they noticed that the people behind the counter were very grouchy. They all looked angry and were snapping at each person when they walked to the counter to get some document. To Bob, this seemed to be the norm in all of the government offices, so it did not surprise him. He knew he was not going up to the counter because he did not speak the language, but Esther was. Bob hoped she did not receive a hard time when it came her turn.

Esther got in line and about one minute after she walked up to the counter, everyone in the whole place was laughing. The more Esther talked the more they all laughed including those waiting in line. The official behind the counter was even acting like it was his privilege to serve Esther, and before long, she had all her papers signed.

Bob stood near the back of the room observing what was happening but having no idea what Esther was saying to bring laughter to everyone in the room. Somehow he was not surprised at what happened because he had seen her take control of situations many times before. When Esther was finished at the counter, she walked out the door, and Bob followed as the people in the room continued laughing.

When they had walked about a block down the street and were in an area with no people around, Bob asked the question, "Esther, what did you say to get everyone laughing like that?" Esther answered, "The Olympics are going on now, so I used that to say I was from Canada, and they were doing very well in hockey, and the Russians were very good too, but the Americans did not know how to play hockey at all. Then I talked about how bad the Americans were playing and how good the Russian hockey team was. (The Americans were doing poorly at that time!) I really elaborated on this, and they all liked it." Bob thought about this for a short time as they continued walking and finally said, "Well Esther, it seemed you were also enjoying it a lot." Esther did not answer, and the two of them went on to their destination.

Through the years, Bob saw an anointing of boldness and wisdom on Esther that was far above what many others had, including him. Then he saw times when she had, what seemed to be, a word of knowledge that was given to her by the Holy Spirit. She also seemed to have an anointing for being fearless in obeying what she felt God was directing her to do. Then Bob watched through the years as hundreds of thousands of dollars came in to support the ministries in which Esther was involved. As Bob added up what God had sent in for all those ministries, it came to a few million dollars. But, the true blessing was that a vast number of people's lives were touched for Jesus Christ through the life of his little girl from the logging camp.

It is almost staggering to Bob as he thinks about these things. He was so fearful when God spoke to him to call Esther and propose marriage, but after being married to her for thirty years, he is so thankful he obeyed. At times, Bob cannot help but wonder how all of this came about in Esther's life. Did God use her hardships to build strength in her to be able to face situations from which many other women would have fled? As Bob thinks about Esther's difficult years and how God blessed her after that, he is reminded of Job's life.

Job 42:12A The LORD *blessed the latter part of Job's life more than the former part.-----(NIV)*

Job went through terrible difficulties because Satan wanted to test him. He did not know that God wanted to prove that Job would remain true to Him no matter what Satan did to him. During the time Satan was testing Job he suffered intensely, yet he remained true to God and the Lord blessed him abundantly in his later years. During Esther's years of struggles she suffered greatly, yet she remained true to God. She also experienced God's faithfulness to her as she went through this difficult period in her life. After this testing time, God blessed and she lived triumphantly in service for her Lord.

After Esther accepted the Lord Jesus Christ as her Savior when she was nine years old, she loved the Lord with all of her heart and delighted herself in Him. Her delight in the Lord was so great that the desire of her heart was to totally serve and obey Him as a missionary. Esther did not even know Psalm 37:4 at that time, but she obeyed the first part of the verse, and God did what He said he would do in the last part and gave her the desire of her heart.

Psalm 37:4 Take delight in the Lord, and he will give you the desires of your heart. (NIV)

Because Esther remained faithful to God through all of her difficulties, He used her to touch the lives of thousands of people for His Son, Jesus Christ. Esther's life verse became a reality in her life. God called Esther when she was very young to be a witness for Him in many places. Then He did what was necessary so she could be obedient to His call. Not only were many souls born-again through her ministry, God also sent a few million dollars to support ministries in which she was involved. The results of this will continue forever.

1 Thessalonians 5:24 The one who calls you is faithful, and he will do it. (NIV)

To this day, the little girl from the logging camp is still living a triumphant life, serving Jesus Christ, both at home and in foreign countries. She has personally witnessed God's faithfulness and her journey in life has been in trusting Him.

Bob McCauley
Dec. 15, 2015